POLE POSITION

JON NICHOLSON
AND MAURICE HAMILTON

POLE POSITION

THE INSIDE STORY OF
WILLIAMS-RENAULT

PAN BOOKS

First published 1995 by Macmillan

This edition published 1996 by Pan Books
an imprint of Macmillan Publishers Ltd
25 Eccleston Place, London SW1W 9NF
and Basingstoke

Associated companies throughout the world

ISBN 0 330 34649 0

1 3 5 7 9 8 6 4 2

A CIP catalogue for this book is available from
the British Library.

Photographic reproduction by Aylesbury Studios, Bromley, Kent
Phototypeset by Intype London Ltd
Printed and bound in Great Britain by
Mackays of Chatham plc, Chatham, Kent

CONTENTS

Introduction vii

1. THE BOYS IN BRAZIL 1

2. ROLLING DOWN THE ROAD 21

3. DOLLAR DRIVEN 43

4. POWER AND PRINT 66

5. TELL ME ABOUT IT 92

6. LIKE TALKING TO MUM 119

7. BRINGING HOME THE BACON 142

8. DOWN HILL IN JAPAN 163

9. IT'S A FUNNY OLD GAME 183

Acknowledgements 196

INTRODUCTION

It is easy to forget that the racing car you see on the track is not just about the man in the cockpit. The driver is an employee, just like everyone else in the team. It so happens that he is taking the company into the limelight for a couple of hours every other weekend during the summer.

The rest of the time, a highly dedicated and hugely talented workforce has made it possible for the driver to be there in the first place. They have worked all hours and any success belongs just as much to the team as it does to the driver. In my case, that means sharing the satisfaction with more than 250 people in the Williams headquarters and the Renault Sports factory.

The trouble is, those behind the scenes are often forgotten in the post-race euphoria. In fact, many spectators have absolutely no idea of the strength and depth of the support which helped to put the driver on to the rostrum. Which is why I am delighted to welcome this book.

Pole Position portrays the tireless efforts and unique skills of the true driving force at Rothmans Williams-Renault. It is the story of the 1995 season, but with the emphasis on various departments and unsung heroes,

∎∎∎∎∎∎∎∎∎∎∎∎∎∎∎∎∎∎∎∎∎∎∎∎∎∎∎∎∎∎∎∎∎∎∎∎∎∎∎

without whom David Coulthard and I would never have made it to the 17 starting grids around the world.

To the best of my knowledge, this sort of book has not been produced before; certainly, not about the activities at Williams and not by two of the most highly qualified authors in motor sport. I can speak from experience because Jon Nicholson and Maurice Hamilton worked with me on the story of my 1994 season, and, once again, their combined talents as photographer and writer have resulted in an accurate and revealing portrayal of a top team fighting for the championship. They had full trust and cooperation and that has been rewarded by a book which pays an excellent tribute to everyone working for a superb team.

DAMON HILL
September 1995

∎∎∎∎∎∎∎∎∎∎∎∎∎∎∎∎∎∎∎∎∎∎∎∎∎∎∎∎∎∎∎∎∎∎∎∎∎∎∎

CHAPTER ONE

THE BOYS IN BRAZIL

BRAZIL AND ARGENTINA

With his overalls rolled down to the waist and his flame-proof vest removed, Damon Hill got down to serious business. Surveying a table to one side of the white-washed room, the winner of the Argentinian Grand Prix finally spotted the item he prized most at that particular moment. After almost two hours' work in humid conditions, then a mouthful of champagne and a lot of talking to the media, there was nothing more welcome than the sight of the Williams teapot. It was, after all, 3.30 on a Sunday afternoon.

In the room next door, Dickie Stanford had beaten Hill to the pour, as the team manager sat quietly to one side and cradled a mug of tea. The euphoria of a convincing win for Rothmans Williams-Renault was still evident but it did little to hide the strain which had been imposed on Stanford during the previous three weeks.

This had been his first spell in charge, an onerous task with which he had become reasonably familiar in his former roles, first as mechanic and then as chief mechanic. During ten years at Williams, Dickie had seen team managers come and go; he knew what it took to marshal the troops and ensure that everything ran as smoothly as could be expected 6,000 miles from home. He had seen it all before, but for this South American trip the responsibility had been his and his after-race exhaustion confirmed the reality.

Stanford had known it would not be easy and the weekend had not disproved this but, as he clasped the blue mug and started to unwind, the notion of doing any other job had not even entered his thoughts. To be a winner in Grand Prix racing requires sacrifice, resilience and the ability to do several things at once. Knowledge, skill and a refusal to panic are taken as read. A team manager is expected to embrace all of these attributes.

He must also have a keen awareness of Grand Prix racing's most precious commodity: money. While the team gets through it at the rate of half a million pounds each week Stanford has to account for every penny spent in his domain. Before the season starts, he must present his budget to team boss Frank Williams, owner and founder of Williams Grand Prix Engineering.

Frank has been in racing since 1964. He remembers only too well the frustration of having unpaid phone bills force the temporary removal of his office to a telephone kiosk across the street. He knows all about the hardships of working on limited resources and has no wish to see his team make a return to living and working hand-to-mouth. That's why his cheque book, although adequately supported, is not easily prised open.

The Williams team has changed beyond recognition since the financial insecurity of the formative days, and Frank intends to keep it that way. Dickie Stanford was made only too aware of this as he accounted for flights, hotels, hire cars, telephone bills and the host of sundry expenses which are incurred while a team of 33 people operates abroad. The pre-race preparation was a major headache long before a racing car had so much as turned a wheel in anger. And then there was the question of freighting the show to Brazil for the first race on 26 March.

While racing in Europe, transportation is taken care of by three trucks and a motor-home. For the so-called 'fly-away' races in South America, Canada, Japan and Australia, everything must be packed in boxes (65 of them on this trip) and carefully weighed.

Each kilogram costs $22 to transport. Freight charges

■ ■

are partially covered by the central fund of the Formula One Constructors' Association, the organization which represents the collective interests of the teams and negotiates matters such as television rights on their behalf. But, even so, leading teams such as Williams need to take another 16 tonnes of freight over and above the FOCA ten-tonne allowance and free shipment of two of the three cars.

Dickie Stanford led an advance party of seven, made up of the truck crews whose job it is at each circuit to set up the garage in preparation for the arrival of the mechanics. The flight to Rome, with an onward connection to Brazil, went smoothly enough but the first hitch came quickly at São Paulo airport. Two of their bags failed to appear. Stanford lost an hour straight away while the matter was sorted out.

However, there was to be compensation for this delay when the first boxes to be delivered to the circuit contained the kit necessary to prepare the Williams garage. With 13 teams and over 1,000 boxes to be taken care of, such good fortune is hard to come by as the FOCA representative, Alan Woollard, attempted to make order of the mountain of equipment being disgorged from the Jumbo freighters.

Each entrant will have been allocated a garage by FOCA, the larger teams sharing extra adjoining garages

■ ■

to allow the spread of equipment. Initial acquaintance with the place of work for the next week reveals bare breeze-block walls, doors front and back and the minimum supply of power, water and, if they are lucky, compressed air. Each team then sets to work, making such rudimentary surroundings seem like home.

Stanford and his crew erected the screens which serve the double purpose of hiding the barren grey walls and providing a useful backdrop for the display of sponsors' names. With the absence of the motor-homes which accompany the teams and engine manufacturers to Europe, temporary offices are built at the back of the garage and areas cordoned off for the positioning of the banks of screens and equipment designed to monitor the cars and engines when out on the track. And, arranged among them somewhere, a place for the catering team and their survival kit, most notably the Williams teapot.

But it is never as simple as that. Stanford had to chase the Brazilian organizers for the generator which had been promised, along with basic equipment for the kitchen. Then there was the installation of telephone and fax lines to see to, and the notification of the numbers to the team headquarters in Didcot.

At the same time that all this had to be organized was the receipt of permanent passes from FOCA for the season,

■ ■

a job often more difficult than extracting blood from a stone and made worse this year by much to-ing and fro-ing between the teams and lawyers over the wording of the contract each team principal was expected to sign before receiving what would always be less than the necessary allocation. There would be enough for the pit crew and management but FOCA cross-examines every request for passes for peripheral figures. Stanford spent hours during the weekend waiting his turn in the queue of increasingly frustrated team managers hoping to enlarge their pass allocations. It was aggravation he did not need.

Such matters were of no interest to Patrick Head, the team's technical director, as he stepped off the London flight on Thursday morning. The mechanics had arrived two days earlier, and by the time Head reached the circuit he would expect to see the cars reassembled and ready for the official scrutineering which precedes every race. But first he would check in to his hotel and take a shower. Then he would expect to find his appropriate passes waiting downstairs at reception, in the same way that he had anticipated a hire car waiting at the airport. Just another of the myriad tasks performed by the team manager in advance.

Stanford, meanwhile, had been busy at the track, checking the location of the race officials' offices (which

■ ■

he would need to visit several times during the course of a weekend that would end in technical disputes), double-check the number of laps in the race, the start time, the precise location of the official speed traps on the circuit so that the team's engineers could make an accurate interpretation of the readings, the nature of the pit lane entry and exit in order to warn the drivers of possible problems and the location of parc ferme where the cars would be held and officially checked and measured at the end of the race.

Then there was the pit stop practice to think about, by no means a matter to be taken lightly. Mechanics enjoy pit stops, up to a point, because they involve them in the race. The buzz that accompanies pit stops for mechanics was offset at the beginning of 1994 when refuelling was introduced. The element of danger was all too evident later that year when the Williams crew witnessed at first hand the inferno engulfing Jos Verstappen, produced by a fault on Benetton's refuelling rig during the German Grand Prix. No one needed reminding that Formula One was fortunate to get away with superficial scorches to the sport's image.

Stanford's need to organize a rehearsal – the latest refuelling rigs had been delivered too late to allow time for a full-dress drill at the Williams factory – was complicated by the fact that he had five new recruits on the race team. The arrival of three of the newcomers had been anticipated but the sudden departure of two crew members one week before the start of the season was another drama the team manager could have done without. Replacements had to be drafted from the team which goes testing rather than racing. The two mechanics would know the new car thanks to an intensive period of testing in Portugal just before the start of the season, but they would not necessarily be au fait with pit stops, a slick procedure which can win or lose races.

Stanford's ambition to have his men finish at a reasonable hour each night (10 p.m., if they were lucky) was compromised by unfamiliarity with the new car, the need to check and double-check each item as well as securing those parts to the car and the allocation of time, once the cars had been completed, to practise pit stops in the shadowy pit lane, the only available light coming through the open garage door.

With the mechanics already having worked flat out either at the factory or at the test track – sometimes both – during the previous fortnight, weariness was understandable and common. Forget the postcard image of shiny new cars simply requiring a polish before being rolled out for the first race.

For Stanford and his team, the only reward would be to see both of their cars on the front row of the grid, proof that the effort had been worthwhile, that Williams Grand Prix Engineering was the best. When the 1995 season kicked off officially at 9.30 on the Friday morning, it was down to the drivers and their respective engineers to get the best out of the mechanics' handiwork.

They came close to being rewarded, Damon Hill starting off his campaign in the best possible way by taking pole position, David Coulthard lining up directly behind his team-mate in third place. Sandwiched between the two Williams-Renaults was their arch-rival, Michael Schumacher, in his Benetton-Renault.

Stanford had been busy throughout, overseeing the team and representing it in debates with the officials. During final qualifying on Saturday afternoon a car had crashed, prompting the appearance of the red flag, a sign that qualifying has been suspended while the wreckage is cleared and that all activity on the track must cease. It so happened that Coulthard was about to complete a fast lap just as the red flag appeared at the start/finish line. It was a close-run thing. Had Coulthard crossed the line fractions of a second earlier, the time recorded on that lap would have counted. And it would have been quicker than anything Coulthard had done before. Stanford made his way to the control tower and argued the point. But the crusty official, a man in his eighties, refused to budge. Rules are rules. Coulthard had not crossed the line before the red

■■

flag had appeared. A tenth of a second might as well have been ten seconds. Nice try all the same, Dickie.

The crew worked late, but not at late as some, the Jordan team finishing at 2.30 a.m., a luxury compared to Benetton, who barely had time to return to the hotel for a shower before making their way back to the track for breakfast and final preparations for the race-morning warm-up at 8.30.

Discussion over the full English breakfast was about one single topic. Word had spread along the pit lane about the inadequacies of the latest refuelling equipment. Two or three teams, when getting down to serious trials for the first time, had experienced fuel leaks. It was the last thing the mechanics needed to hear. The Williams team was not alone in formulating a procedure which would call for caution, despite the need for speed. Absolutely no risks would be taken. Better to have a delay than a pit ravaged by fire. But who needed such a threat in a sport which was already bristling with potential hazards?

Stanford had been re-reading the sporting regulations. He had to know them by heart because, in the heat of the moment, there would not be time to find and consult the document, make a decision and issue instructions. If, say, the race was stopped because of an accident before the end of two laps, he had to know straightaway that this would call for a fresh start, in original grid positions,

■■

with the race distance the same as before and the topping up of fuel permitted on the grid. If the Grand Prix was stopped once two laps had passed, then the race was definitely on and he had to know that different rules would apply.

In the event of a query which required a quick answer, all eyes would turn to the team manger. And God help him if he got it wrong; one false move and the car – perhaps both cars – could be excluded. Stomach cramps had ensured that Stanford hadn't been sleeping well at night but he wouldn't be able to sleep at all if he made a blunder of that magnitude. The lads would not have to express their feelings about wasted effort. Stanford had been there. He knew all about the anger and frustration which would suddenly burst forth.

In fact, there would be tension on Sunday, but it would strike late in the day. The first hint had come just before the start. Stanford had been handed an official note informing Williams that the fuel, taken from Coulthard's car after practice on Friday, did not match an approved sample submitted before the start of the season by the team's supplier, Elf.

Coulthard's times from Friday were therefore annulled, not that it made any difference to his grid position since his best lap had been established the following day. But the implications were obvious. Elf would be using the same fuel for the race and if, at the end of it, another sample was taken in parc ferme and the same conclusion reached, then the car would be excluded from the results.

Stanford had to take all this on board at a time when pulses were racing as the final count-down got into its dramatic stride. Consulting Frank Williams straight away, Stanford was wisely told to concentrate on the race. There was nothing which could be done about the fuel at this stage; they would worry about the fuel check later.

Stanford positioned himself by the pit wall, his head-set tuned to both drivers' frequencies. Radio communications between the driver and his engineer during the race would be brief and for emergency only, the drivers relying on messages displayed on the boards hung over the wall each time the cars blasted past the pits. Nonetheless, if there was a problem, Stanford had to hear about it.

The early part of the race was routine from the team manager's point of view. Hill was beaten to the first corner by Schumacher with Coulthard respectfully staying in third place. Despite a couple of attempts by Hill to get by, the positions remained the same until Hill moved ahead once he got a clear track after Schumacher had dived into the pits for his first refuelling stop.

Hill's pit stop followed soon after, and there were none of the anticipated problems with the refuelling equipment. Damon's fast laps were good enough to give him a lead which he seemed unlikely to lose.

Then came brief messages across the head-set. Hill was having trouble with the semi-automatic gearbox. The Williams-Renault crossed the line for the thirtieth time; that was the last the team would see of it. As Hill swept into the downhill section at the end of the pit straight, the rear suspension, pounded unmercilessly by a dreadfully bumpy track, suddenly broke and pitched the car onto the grass, where the disgruntled driver climbed out and walked away.

Now Coulthard had the team's full attention as he maintained a steady second place, intent on giving the Williams lads something to show for a long weekend's work. In fact, as the time for the second pit stop approached, it seemed to the pit crew that Coulthard might be able to take the lead, but that plan collapsed when the Williams failed to appear in the pit lane at the precise moment everyone had anticipated.

By half-climbing onto the pit wall and peering towards the pit entrance, Stanford could see the cause of the trouble. A Jordan was being pushed into the pit lane and Coulthard was trapped behind it. The six seconds lost would be enough to keep the Williams in second place as Coulthard rejoined. That was the end of the challenge.

Second place was the minimum a team such as

Williams would expect. But at the end of a punishing prelude to the season, it was better than nothing. Now the objective was to take everything down in the garage, pack the boxes and get out of Brazil as quickly as possible. Stanford and the mechanics were due to leave for Argentina the following day; the drivers and team management were already on their way to the hotel to shower, change and catch a flight back to Britain.

As darkness closed in, Stanford was working in the rapidly disintegrating garage. A journalist appeared and asked Dickie if he knew the result. Thinking the man to be totally incompetent, Stanford replied that of course he knew the result: Schumacher first, David Coulthard second, the Ferrari of Gerhard Berger third.

'No, no,' said the journalist. 'The latest result. There's a problem with the Elf fuel used by Benetton and Williams. You may be excluded.'

Stanford froze on the spot. He knew that fuel samples had been taken as a matter of course but this was the first sign of trouble. Not long after, an official came into the garage and told Stanford he was not to leave the circuit, pending the result of the check on the fuel.

Dickie grabbed a phone and called the hotel. Frank Williams had already left but Stanford managed to catch Patrick Head just as he was checking out.

After much deliberation, the technical delegate finally

declared that the fuel used by Schumacher and Coulthard did not match the original sample submitted by Elf and approved pre-season by the sport's governing body, the Fédération Internationale de l'Automobile (FIA). Both drivers were excluded from the results; Gerhard Berger had become the winner of the Brazilian Grand Prix.

This was the final straw for the beleaguered mechanics as they sifted through the equipment and packed it away. And then, to add to Stanford's problems, a local man, who had been employed as a so-called 'gofer', ran into trouble at the exit gate.

The team had been forced to spend £2,000 on a hefty three-phase electrical cable to help feed the power to the garage. Since there would be no need for the cable at any of the following races and the freight home would be an unnecessary expense, it made sense to have the gofer keep it for the following year. The security guards thought the man was stealing the cable and not even a note on Williams paper, signed by Stanford, would persuade them otherwise. It required the team manager, armed with his passport, to go all the way to the front gate and convince the security men that everything was in order. And all of this in the midst of the tension over having a car disqualified.

An exhausted Stanford got back to the hotel at 11 p.m., went straight to his room and ordered coffee and a club

■■■

sandwich. The next thing he knew was the sound of
the waiter beating on the door. Having eaten, Stanford
collapsed back into instant slumber. He awoke in the
morning, still fully clothed.

There was much still to be done. While the rest of the
Formula One circus remaining in Brazil went into cruise
mode and for the first time enjoyed a leisurely breakfast,
Stanford was on the phone to the Williams headquarters
in England, sorting out the repercussions of the stewards'
decision.

Then there was the hotel bill to be settled, a mammoth
task considering it was the team manager's job to take
care of the some of the sponsors' rooms as well as his
team of mechanics' and ensure that the sponsors would
later be re-charged. Then there was the return of the hire
cars, some of which had been left at the airport in the
rush to catch flights the previous evening. But where were
the cars exactly? And what had happened to the keys?
Stanford had instructed everyone on precisely what to do,
but in the confusion of a busy airport departures area . . .
well, you know how it is: 'I'll just leave the car here –
Dickie can sort it out.'

Damon Hill's car could not be found. What on earth
had he done with it? In fact, Damon had left the car
exactly where he had been told; such cooperation caught
everyone unawares. Finally, Stanford had to ensure that

■■

the boxes were gathered together at the circuit, ready for shipment. Then the mechanics had to be bussed to the airport and checked in. So much for Brazil. What would Argentina have in store the following morning?

Not a lot, as things turned out. The team landed in Buenos Aires, only to find that the hire cars were at a different airport. Once at the hotel, Stanford then discovered that most of the bedrooms were not available. And those that were free had not been made up. Alternative arrangements were made which saw the lads sharing double beds or sleeping on camp beds; they were so tired that anything was acceptable in the interim.

The following day, Wednesday, Stanford spent nearly three hours in the hotel manager's office, watching rooms come free on the computer and grabbing them immediately before the front desk snapped them up for other clients. With the mechanics finally installed in their twin-bedded rooms, the hotel laundry managed to lose team shirts and those that were not lost spent between three and four days going through the supposedly 'same-day' system.

On Thursday of the following week came the start of the rain which would last for most of the race weekend. Two mechanics had to switch rooms again when they returned to find water cascading down the bedroom wall. Some of the hire vehicles had to be abandoned when the windscreen wipers failed to work and the rain reached torrential proportions. And just for good measure, a rogue fire alarm had everyone on the top few floors evacuate their rooms.

On Wednesday and Thursday the management flew in from England, but last-minute changes to flight plans kept Stanford on his toes as he organized the waiting hire cars with maps and the two-pesos fee for the motorway toll. In between, he had to provide details to the FOCA office in London of the trucks and motor-homes the team intended to take to the next race at Imola in Italy. And he had to think about preparing a truck in the latest colour scheme – complete with all the sponsors' names – in order to go testing immediately after the Argentinian Grand Prix.

Apart from the usual boxes flown in from Brazil, there were two additional items of freight being shipped from the factory and containing replacement parts and modifications to the cars. And there was the usual South American problem of having at least one mechanic confined to the bathroom with, to put it kindly, stomach trouble.

The Buenos Aires track had not hosted the Grand Prix for fourteen years and the last-minute preparations had found the garage floors still being laid as teams arrived to set up shop. There were no lights and no power. Tables, chairs and fridges had to be organized for the white-washed rooms which would provide the base for the kitchen and working facilities for the management from Williams and Renault. But, at $3,000 per room for the weekend, these very basic comforts did not come cheap. The absence of telephone lines meant the team had to hire mobile phones until more permanent communications had been established. And, when they were, Stanford probably wished the entire phone network would grind to a halt as calls at £6 per minute ate even further into his budget. Would it be worth the trouble and expense?

There was no question about the answer as Damon Hill, grinning from ear to ear, reached for the pot of tea at 3.30 on Sunday afternoon. He had not only won the race but overtaken Schumacher to do it. David Coulthard had done the same to the Benetton but the chances of a one-two for Williams were wiped out when throttle trouble meant it was the Scotsman's turn to sit on the sidelines.

Hill had won without the rancour provoked by the post-race scrutineering in Brazil (whose exclusions would be overturned on appeal the week after the Argentinian Grand Prix). The South American phase was over. All Stanford had to do now was sort out the hotel bills – not the work of a moment as he unravelled all the room changes, the late arrivals and the early departures.

After three weeks away from his wife, Lorraine, and his two daughters, Jennifer and Lucinda, Stanford would be lucky if there was a day, maybe two, free to spend at home in the small village outside Swindon while the freight winged its way to Heathrow. Then it would be down to business once more. Never mind that the following weekend was Easter. No one said motor racing was a holiday.

CHAPTER TWO

ROLLING DOWN
THE ROAD

SAN MARINO AND SPAIN

The comparison was extreme. Five weeks after Damon
Hill had celebrated with the teapot in Buenos Aires, he
cut a lonely and forlorn figure at the end of the Spanish
Grand Prix. As his Williams coasted across the finishing
line, there was not a single member of the team at the
pit wall to greet him.

The Williams crew were already busying themselves
with the tidying up operation, the management grouped
at the back of the garage studying the telemetry, trying
to understand why Damon had slowed so dramatically on
the last lap. He had started it safe in second place – a
reasonable result considering the problems Williams had
encountered during practice and the drubbing dealt out
by Michael Schumacher and the victorious Benetton team

– but suddenly he was fourth as Herbert and Berger rushed past to gratefully accept the elevation to second and third.

The hydraulic pump having failed, Hill was struggling to reach the finish with a dead engine, the Williams rolling down the hill to the line before finally pulling onto the grass. Damon flicked off his seat belts and levered himself from the cockpit after an hour and 36 minutes of hard endeavour. Easing off his helmet, removing his flameproof balaclava and unpicking the tape holding his earplugs-cum-radio speakers in place, Hill walked to the concrete wall, heaved himself across it and dropped into the pit lane.

The frustration of the moment was compounded by the sight of the Benetton team celebrating not only a well-deserved victory but also the unexpected bonus of a clean sweep as Herbert stole Hill's second place. Next door, there was silence in the Williams garage, save for the clatter of equipment being cleared away. Hill walked quickly through without saying a word, the mechanics not daring to meet his dark scowl.

Fourth place. What use was that? The three-point difference between second and fourth had cost him the lead of the championship. It could be crucial when the points were totted up at the end of the year; in 1994, Hill had lost the title to Schumacher by a single point. The Spanish result was a disaster for Williams on a day when David Coulthard's car had retired with a bearing failure in the gearbox.

All of this was relative. There were teams, struggling to survive at the lower end of the pit lane, who would have killed for fourth place. But, for Williams, being first of the also-rans was highly unsatisfactory, particularly as their world had just been turned upside down following a brilliant win for Hill two weeks before in the San Marino Grand Prix at Imola. Benetton had been in trouble there, Schumacher crashing out of the lead. Now they had recovered and it was Williams who had been taking the stick in this, the fourth round of the championship.

It was hard on everyone, not least the truck drivers as they prepared for the long run home from Barcelona. As likely as not, they would reach the French coast, board the ferry to Dover, sit down in the lorry drivers' café and face the usual banter about having had a week off in the Spanish sun. The barbed remarks would be based partly on ignorance of the complexity of the role played by the Grand Prix truckies and partly on jealousy over their equipment.

Being in partnership with Renault means Williams has access to some of the best tractor units on the road. And, along with the brightly coloured transporters, they are always immaculately presented. In terms of road haulage, the race teams represent the Rolls-Royce brigade, a target for taunts by drivers entrusted with more mundane vehicles and less glamorous work. The Williams truckies could understand the feelings of barely muted resentment but that didn't make life any easier at the end of a week-end which had brought little in terms of the level of success to which the Rothmans Williams-Renault team had become accustomed.

Ironically, victory for Hill and fourth place for Coul-thard in Italy two weeks before merely served to aggravate the sense of failure in Spain. These two races had marked the opening of the European season and, if nothing else, their diverse nature had indicated to the team that 1995 looked like being as competitive as ever. With a race roughly once a fortnight from now until the end of September, the hard grind of the season was under way.

With the South American 'fly-away' races over and done with, the San Marino Grand Prix marked the first appearance this season of the transporters and motor-homes. These purpose-designed vehicles would provide a home-from-home where team members could carry on their business with maximum efficiency and minimum disruption.

The two articulated transporters and the rigid-axle truck transport 14 tons of equipment to each race. They also serve as travelling extensions of the factory floor. The three race cars are carried together in the truck which has double decks designed specifically for that purpose. The other two vehicles take care of the vast array of spare bodywork, wings, computers, trolleys, wheel rims, generators, jacks, air guns, air lines, refuelling equipment, flameproof overalls for the pit crew on race day, garage backcloths, signalling gear, radios and head-sets and the tubular pit stand for the team management to work from when the cars are out on the track.

The small tools, accessories and sundry items are stored in multi-drawer units resembling kitchen fitments running down either side of each truck. Rather than have the mechanics dash to and from the transporter each time a spanner is required, some of the units can be unbolted and wheeled into place in the garage, adding to the general appearance of efficiency and professionalism.

Ten years ago, Williams, in keeping with other top teams, relied on just one articulated truck and a box van. In 1995, the plethora of equipment brought on by increasingly high standards of presentation and technology dictated the need for three vehicles and a crew of six truckies. Simon Peters and Keith Biddick took care of the transporter with the race cars, Steve Coates and Chris Newcombe looked after the second articulated truck, which carried the spares as well as providing, at one end, a debrief room for the drivers and engineers, while the smaller rigid vehicle, carrying the heavy and cumbersome refuelling equipment, was in the hands of Jimmy Walters and Colin Hessey.

Having spent the weekend before Imola loading and packing, the trucks left Didcot at 5 p.m. on the Sunday and headed for Portsmouth. The overnight sailing berthed in Le Havre at 6.30 a.m., the crews taking four-hour shifts at the wheel to reach the night halt at Chamonix. With border controls more relaxed in these unified times, the target of reaching Imola in northern Italy by mid-afternoon on Tuesday was easily attained.

There had been times, however, when an eight-hour wait would not have been unusual at the Mont Blanc crossing into Italy, the teams at the mercy of customs officials as they frequently over-exercised their rights by emptying each truck. The prize was not contraband items – not that they would have found any – but team gear such as uniforms and stickers. The value of bartering items in return for a swift passage was soon lost as officials expected presents as a matter of routine. It was not until the teams made an unofficial pact not to carry any souvenirs that the practice stopped. However, the initial period of gift-free running led to many an unwanted delay until the message finally got across.

If the transporters' journey to Imola had been trouble-free, the same could not be said for the maiden voyage of the new motor-home, commissioned by Williams for the start of the 1995 European season. The Renault bus had to be tailored to suit the specialized requirements of the team, with meeting rooms, a kitchen, shower and a lift to allow Frank Williams access in his wheelchair. As with everything associated with Grand Prix racing, the conversion of the motor-home was a last-minute rush job. Quite how rushed would only become evident when Dickie Stanford, the team manager, and Paul Edwards, the motor-home driver and team chef, went to the coach builders in Andover to oversee what should have been the final touches of the transformation.

In fact, because of delays in choosing the final specification, the work had hardly started. Stanford and Edwards spent four days in the workshop, Paul providing tea, sandwiches and support, Dickie doing his best to ensure that the job was completed as specified. On Saturday evening, Stanford sent Paul home to rest and gave the conversion company the ultimatum that the motor-home had to be ready in time to leave on Sunday lunchtime. Some hope. As Sunday midnight approached, the job was nowhere near completion. Edwards said he would rest for a few hours – and then he simply had to leave with the motor-home, whatever state it was in.

He awoke at 4.30 a.m. on Monday morning. And still

the work was continuing. Paul went over the vehicle with the electrician, checked out details such as the fitting of the satellite dish, and generally found his way around what would be his home and workplace for the next six months as he criss-crossed Europe – that's assuming he ever reached the San Marino Grand Prix to kick off the summer campaign.

Edwards started the engine of the motor-home at 8 a.m. This was it – he was leaving *now* and if those on board were not finished, then too bad. According to the schedule, he should have been parking in the paddock at Imola. He was 24 hours late. Valuable time could be saved by using the Channel tunnel and Edwards got on the phone to Donna Robertson, the travel coordinator at the Williams headquarters. The booking was made but Edwards was destined never to get on that train.

As Paul and his assistant, Michael Meredith, pulled into the car park at the Folkestone terminal, the motor-home's engine cut out. A quick check led Paul to believe that the problem was caused by an air lock in the diesel supply. Burying himself in the engine bay at the rear of the coach, Edwards had been working for several minutes when, to his horror, the engine suddenly turned over.

Meredith, not realizing Edwards was still up to his armpits in machinery, had decided to give the starter one more try. He was too far forward to hear Paul's anguished yell as the tips of two fingers on his left hand were sliced off by the cogged drive belts of the air conditioning.

Horror-struck when he realized Edwards's plight, Michael called an ambulance. When the terminal's first-aid man arrived to see what could be done, he took one look at the damaged fingers – and promptly keeled over. But the Chunnel authorities and the RAC kept a cool head and took great care of Edwards before he was rushed to the nearby hospital in Ashford where, later that evening, an operation, involving a skin graft from his hip, was successfully carried out.

Meredith, meanwhile, was instructed to carry on. To add to his anguish, the hydraulic clutch began to give trouble; the maiden voyage of the motor-home seemed doomed. As a precaution, its predecessor, which still happened to be at the Williams factory, was dispatched as a back-up. In the event, it would not be needed. Michael arrived safely at Imola on Tuesday, not long after the truck drivers had begun to unload and set up the garages allocated to Williams-Renault.

This would be a difficult weekend for the team, coming, as it did, exactly one year after Ayrton Senna had died at this very circuit at the wheel of a Williams. Stepping into the long narrow paddock brought the terrible memories streaming back for the team members, the majority of whom had never before known tragedy –

certainly not as close as this – in motor racing. The risk factor had always been there, of course, but on 1 May 1994, the terrible reality of their business had been horribly confirmed. Each member of the team would deal with the weekend in their own private way, culminating in a brief but moving gathering at the deserted accident scene on Saturday evening. In the meantime, there was a race to be won.

Having unloaded his truck and played his part in setting up the garage, Steve Coates focused on his other area of responsibility, wheels and tyres. Preparation had begun at the factory, with the best part of three days having been spent X-raying, crack-testing, cleaning and checking the mileage on the hundred or so wheel rims necessary for the San Marino Grand Prix weekend.

The tyres themselves are brought to each race by Goodyear, Formula One's sole supplier. Williams, in common with the leading teams, has a contract with Goodyear which allows for free supply, but the smaller teams have to pay £350 for each tyre. The financial arrangements were of no concern to Steve Coates as he deposited the wheel rims in the Goodyear compound to await the mounting of the tyres.

The rapid pace of tyre development during recent decades led to the appearance of treadless 'slick' tyres whose sole object is to provide maximum grip. Since each team would be supplied with identical tyres, a successful tyre performance would depend on the correct pressure for the occasion and the rubber reaching its optimum working temperature of around 100°C. That burden of responsibility would rest with Steve Coates.

Each driver would be limited to twenty-eight tyres throughout the weekend (with the exception of treaded rain tyres, which would be unrestricted). How and when those tyres would be used would be at the whim of the driver and his engineer but, either way, Coates had to make sure that each tyre was marked with the driver's race number by the scrutineer so that the car could be inspected each time it left the pit lane, to check that the driver was using only the tyres he had been allocated. Coates would also ensure that each tyre was mounted the correct way round. Unlike the tyres on a road car – which can run in either direction – for optimum performance a racing tyre must rotate in a specified direction in order to match the way in which the rubber has been laid during manufacture.

Then the various sets of four tyres had to be numbered, Hill taking the odd numbers, Coulthard the even, to help avoid confusion. It would be necessary to make a swift identification once practice got underway and the drivers began 'scrubbing' the tyres they hoped to race. The process of scrubbing (quickly bringing the rubber up to temperature and then removing the tyres from the car) would help cure the rubber and prolong the performance and longevity of the tyres in the race. Some sets of tyres would feel better than others and the drivers would need to have them easily identified.

During qualifying, however, the tyres would be run from new, the optimum performance coming within the second or third laps, before dropping off. The abuse delivered during those few laps would more or less render the tyre useless for the endurance required for the race; hence the process of scrubbing race tyres and then setting them aside until Sunday.

Coates would also be making sure that the tyre pressures were as ordered by the driver and his engineer; not as simple as it sounds when you consider that pressures can vary by as much as 9 p.s.i. between cold and hot. If the engineer requests pressures of, say, 22 and 18 p.s.i. front and rear, then the tyre man has to ensure he is within 1 p.s.i. of that. Any discrepancy will upset the balance of the car and make the accurate and efficient setting up of the suspension and aerodynamics impossible.

Assistance comes in the form of tyre warmers, electric blankets which heat the rubber at 85°C for two hours before use. This process, where the tyres are stacked, wrapped in their blankets, with portable generators providing the electrical power, also allows the heat to sink into the wheel rim itself, thus making the final setting of the pressure easier, although Coates would also have to take into account the fierce heat from the brakes which would enter the wheels – and hence increase the tyre pressure.

In fact, that is one of many variables which must be considered. An abrasive track surface can increase tyre pressure initially, just as much as a worn tyre can eventually reduce it. The weight of fuel carried on board the car can have a bearing on tyre wear and, similarly, a change in track temperature caused by sudden cloud cover can cause pressures to drop by 1.5 p.s.i. And, throughout all this, the driver will expect his tyre pressures to be correct, regardless of whether he is engaged in the flat-out two- or three-lap blind of qualifying or a concentrated run of twenty laps during practice or the race itself.

When practice and qualifying have finished, the tyre men must set aside the race tyres which have been scrubbed and allow them to cool overnight. The tyres will be checked for cuts, and the rims inspected for damage. Stripes, placed by marker pen and running from the rim and onto the tyre, will be examined to ensure that the tyre has not moved on the rim thanks to the fierce forces exerted under braking as the car slows from 180 to

70 m.p.h. in less than 1.5 seconds. If the tyre has moved, even by the smallest fraction, then the wheel will have to be rebalanced.

The rims will be washed and the balance weights checked. And, always, the final check will be to ensure that the valve caps are in place. On a Grand Prix car, the centrifugal forces are such that if the cap is missing the air inside the tyre will lift the valve from its seat and gradually thrust its way out.

But such routine matters were the least of Steve Coates's worries as race day dawned at Imola. He faced the worst conundrum of all; a wet start with the possibility of the the track drying out. There would almost certainly be changes from grooved wet-weather tyres to slicks. The tyre pressures on the 'wets' would be relatively straight-forward. But guessing the conditions – the track surface, the ambient temperature, the fuel load which might be on board – when the slicks would be required was almost a lottery, which tyre men throughout the pit lane would be expected to get right to the last p.s.i.

The Williams equation was not helped by the fact that neither car was on the front row of the grid for the first time since Monza, the previous September. David Coulthard had qualified third, with Damon Hill fourth, both drivers, in keeping with the rest of the field, having been frustrated by slower track conditions during final qualifying, a period when everyone, not least the Williams drivers, had expected to improve their position. For Hill, this was even more frustrating than usual because he knew his car felt good; good enough to win – provided his race tactics were sound. Provided the tyre pressures were correct.

As the race got underway with Schumacher leading from Berger's Ferrari, Coulthard and Hill were in third and fourth places, fine plumes of spray rising from the grooved tyres. But the rain stopped and it was a question of how soon it would be before the leaders would want to change to slicks. It so happened that a large proportion of the Imola circuit had been resurfaced (due to revisions to the layout in the interests of safety), which meant the track conditions were virtually unknown under circumstances such as these.

However, Coates noted that the surface was not drying as quickly as might have been anticipated. It meant that, all things being equal, the drivers would stop for slicks while the track was still damp – but the racing line would not become dry for several laps after that. Hence the slick tyres would run cooler than expected and the tyre pressures would not rise in their customary manner. With no time to dither – Berger was already making his way down the pit lane for slick tyres after just six laps – Coates

■■■■■■■■■■■■■■■■■■■■■■■■■■■■■■■■■■■■■

took a gamble and squirted another 1.5 p.s.i. into the slicks waiting for Coulthard and Hill.

It was the perfect decision, Hill finding his car beautifully balanced as he settled into the chase. Hill's cause was helped no end when Schumacher, under intense pressure, crashed heavily after spinning off the greasy track. Berger then disappeared out of the lead when making an early stop for his third set of tyres, and Hill was home and, as the sun began to ease through, more or less dry.

It was a brilliant win for Hill. He remained calm in the early stages and then hammered home the advantage of a car – and tyres – which were performing brilliantly. After an adventurous race in which he spun and cost himself more time by earning a ten-second penalty for exceeding the pit lane speed limit, David Coulthard finished fourth. Williams were heading the Constructors' Championship and, for the first time ever, Damon Hill was leading the World Championship by six points from Schumacher.

Paul Edwards had watched qualifying and the race with the factory-based personnel at Didcot. With his fingers still gently throbbing, Edwards was astonished to hear his name mentioned on Eurosport, commentator John Watson making reference to the injury and, somewhat strangely, a packet of chocolate fingers. It was a pre-planned job prepared in collusion with the team who presented Edwards with the chocolate fingers – which

■■■■■■■■■■■■■■■■■■■■■■■■■■■■■■■■■■■■

• •

were broken after the packet had been deliberately dropped on the floor.

Despite his painful setback, Edwards would have been
the first to agree that things were going Williams's way.
Steve Coates and his colleagues certainly felt that way as
they managed to spot no less than four radar traps – not
that the truckies were speeding, of course – on the journey
home.

Seven days later, the blue and white transporters were
heading through France once more, this time en route to
Barcelona, one of the toughest journeys on the Grand Prix
schedule. Having unloaded at Didcot and gone through
the usual routine of checking and sorting the wheel
rims, the crews had to have the transporters packed and
ready to go, the three refettled racing cars on board, by
Monday morning. After a night's rest in France, the fifteen-
hour run had the three trucks taking their pre-allocated
parking places in the Circuit de Catalunya paddock by
Tuesday evening. On Wednesday morning, the drivers
threw open the truck doors and started the process all
over again.

There was no reason to believe that Williams could not
continue their dominance. Benetton were clearly on the
run, Schumacher's uncharacteristically ragged driving a
sign that he was under pressure with a car which did
not handle well – or, certainly, not as competently as the

• •

■ ■

Williams. But Frank Williams and his team had been in the game long enough to realize that nothing lasts for ever. Even so, the speed of change in Spain was to catch everyone by surprise. And the first hint, significantly, was connected with tyres.

Hill and Coulthard were in trouble on the first day of practice, neither driver particularly happy with the handling of the Williams. But at least Benetton were not much better off and Williams buckled down to serious work on Friday evening as they looked at ways of improving the car in time for final qualifying. When Hill and Coulthard then set the fastest times during unofficial practice on Saturday morning, all seemed set fair for an all-Williams front row when final qualifying took place a couple of hours later.

Schumacher had been third quickest, half a second away from Hill and seemingly no threat. But Hill was worried. Walking from the garage, Damon bumped into Alan Henry, the journalist gathering information for the official news bulletin. 'Was Schumacher on fresh tyres?' asked Hill. When Henry said no, Hill's dark brow developed another furrow or two. 'That's bad news then,' mused Hill, 'because I was.'

The inference was clear. If Schumacher had set his time without the benefit of fresh rubber – worth at least half a second a lap – then there would be more to come when

■ ■

he fitted new tyres during qualifying. Benetton had been doing their homework and come up with a few answers. According to Hill, the Williams was much better than before – but Benetton seemed to have made a massive stride.

The stunning proof of that came when Schumacher took pole and lapped the Circuit de Catalunya almost a second faster than Hill. Worse still, Alesi and Berger had put their Ferraris between the Benetton and Coulthard's fourth-place Williams. For only the second time since he had joined the Williams race team at the beginning of 1993, Damon Hill had qualified outside the top four. Such an impressive record was no consolation whatsoever. Hill had come to Barcelona concerned about the rise in competitiveness of the Ferraris. Overnight, Benetton had overtaken everyone. This race would be far from easy.

Sure enough, after a quick getaway, Schumacher simply disappeared into a race of his own. But Hill made the most of a good start while Coulthard's excellent work during practice was negated by the inefficiency of the starting system. The routine is to have the field complete a final parade lap, form up on the grid and, when everyone is in place, a signal from the back of the grid informs the starter that he can proceed.

The official then switches on the red lights, followed, between three and seven seconds later, by the green. On

▪▪▪▪▪▪▪▪▪▪▪▪▪▪▪▪▪▪▪▪▪▪▪▪▪▪▪▪▪▪▪▪▪▪▪▪▪▪

this occasion, the starter did that – but the green lights never appeared. Grand Prix drivers are nothing if not opportunists, the majority choosing to go as soon as the red lights began to fade rather than wait for the green. David Coulthard was waiting for the green when the rest of the field took off. He was immediately sixth, with plenty of work to do. Hill, meanwhile, was third and ready to take advantage of Jean Alesi's departure when the Ferrari retired from second place with engine failure.

Going into the last lap, Hill was satisfied with second place. The car had not been anything like as good as he would have wished and Coulthard had retired when a bearing in the gearbox had failed. This was worrying because David had been forced out of the Argentinian Grand Prix by the excessive vibrations on the electronics control box and Damon's suspension had broken in Brazil. Now this.

The team had experienced a similar bearing failure during testing. But it had been in a gearbox with high mileage and the problem had been put down to a question of old age. The gearbox on Coulthard's car had been new for the weekend. So much for that theory. Coming away with six points would be a reasonable enough result for Williams.

As Hill sped down the straight on his last lap and went to change up from fifth to sixth, nothing happened. The

▪▪▪▪▪▪▪▪▪▪▪▪▪▪▪▪▪▪▪▪▪▪▪▪▪▪▪▪▪▪▪▪▪▪▪▪▪▪

pump operating the hydraulics had chosen to fail with less than three miles to go. The team had never experienced such a failure before. The semi-automatic gearbox, driven by hydraulics and operated by the driver pulling levers mounted behind the steering wheel spokes, was stuck in fifth gear.

No matter. Hill could chug along without too much problem. Or he could have done, had the same hydraulic pump not operated the throttle mechanism as well. In times of trouble, the system tells the throttle to shut itself down (for fear of sticking open and causing all manner of mayhem) and Hill now found himself with the engine on tick over. Eventually, it did not even do that. As the final corner (fortunately, it was downhill) came into view, the engine died completely. With the gearbox still stuck in fifth, Hill jammed his foot on the clutch to allow the car to freewheel – ever so slowly. By now, Herbert and Berger had rushed by to take second and third. Since Hill had lapped everyone else, his new-found fourth place was safe, even if he failed to complete the last lap. But Damon was not to know that and, under the circumstances, he did the right thing by attempting to coax the now-silent car across the line.

He made it. Just. But after 65 punishing laps, his left leg, still pushing hard on the clutch, had developed severe cramp. As Hill pulled onto the grass by the pit wall he was in agony. And there was not a friendly face to greet him.

CHAPTER THREE

DOLLAR DRIVEN

MONACO AND CANADA

On the eve of the Monaco Grand Prix, two very different dinners took place in the principality; one under a PVC awning, close by a shabby warehouse on the quayside, and the other in a glitzy restaurant a few yards from the Hôtel de Paris. Both were organized by Formula One teams as a means of entertaining guests. One was hugely successful and the other an expensive shambles.

The temporary accommodation by the harbour won hands down, a fact which did not surprise Richard West in the least since he had engineered it. As commercial director at Williams, West has a keen appreciation of value for money, both from the team's point of view and the sponsor's. Monaco may be Grand Prix racing's showcase, a place for the flaunting of wealth, but in these times of financial constraint no team can afford to be profligate.

The industry high-rollers the teams seek to attract did not get to their positions of eminence by being careless with their cash. The job of West and his marketing team of ten is to convince prospective partners that Williams and Grand Prix racing together make a sound investment; that anything from £100,000 for a low-key involvement to £1m and more as a major sponsor is money well spent. And, more to the point, once the deal has been agreed, this is an investment which is suitably and uniquely rewarded. Monaco, with its attendant glamour, is the perfect place to do that. But you need to get your sums right in every respect.

The problem is that *everyone* wants to be there. West has to convince his clients that quality, not quantity, is the only solution. Bring a few people – preferably the most influential and important – and they will be treated royally. Arrive mob-handed, and it will be impossible to cater for everyone's needs; someone is bound to be disappointed.

Monaco, because of the temporary nature of the circuit and the tight restriction on passes, is a logistical nightmare. This is not a traditional circuit in the sense that the helicopter pad is over there, the car park a quick step away, the hospitality suite right here, the pits down below; everything in easy reach.

At Monaco, moving from A to B requires a packed lunch and a compass. Simply finding a loo is a major achievement. Attempting to shepherd important visitors around the place is like walking barefoot and blindfolded in the London rush hour. West and his team are aware of the pitfalls – hence the seemingly unusual location for the pre-race dinner for Rothmans Middle East and a handful of key journalists from that part of the world.

West reasoned that any restaurant in Monte Carlo on Saturday night would be a heaving scrum. Unwittingly, another Formula One team – which had better remain anonymous to save embarrassment – proved his point by taking the same number of guests (20) to an ostensibly smart establishment, all chrome and bright lights, where Iranian Beluga caviare – as an hors-d'oeuvre – cost £120. All very nice but such extravagance quickly loses its appeal when the first course takes an hour and a quarter to appear and the main course, when it finally arrives, is either the wrong order or hastily prepared. The meal ran so late that guests were refused coffee because the tables were needed for the next party.

Meanwhile, in more serene surroundings down on the quay, a silver-service dinner outside the motor-home saw five girls quickly and efficiently serve food cooked by the

Rothmans chef. Damon Hill popped in to say hello and David Coulthard took turns to sit at each table and chat to the guests.

When the meal was over, the party was invited to move under the awning next door and watch the Williams mechanics make final late-night preparations for the race. The unique sense of exclusivity, of being part of this great team, was priceless. And there was no risk of being prevented from returning to the dinner table for coffee and liqueurs.

The key to it all was the provision of an experience the guests would never forget. It was a theme which would run throughout the weekend as the Williams marketing department took care of an often ignored aspect of their game: the business of servicing the client once the deal has been agreed.

'Servicing is one of the key points,' agrees West. 'When talking to a prospective partner, we sell three things: the value of Williams Grand Prix Engineering in terms of the team's history, technical ability and exposure; Formula One, and what it offers from the point of view of global exposure, television statistics and the increasing of brand awareness; and, finally, the servicing we provide throughout the duration of the contract. I think people assume we take the money and then go to the track, have lunch, watch the Grand Prix and go home. We're lucky if we have time to grab a sandwich on race day.'

At Monaco, West and his team appeared to eat nothing but two-way radios. Communications were vital because the sponsors and their guests were spread throughout various locations. Williams were responsible for 140 people from Rothmans, 100 from Renault, 20 from Elf, four VIPs from the coffee suppliers Segafredo, a handful from the Reh Group, a German company which owns Black Tower wine, and six chief executives from companies taking a look at Grand Prix racing with an eye to future sponsorship involvement.

Popular imagery has it that boats provide the romantic setting for such gatherings but the reality is quite different. It doesn't take much of a breeze to create a swell in the harbour, a situation which does little for the digestive system and the general feeling of wellbeing. Besides, the view is hampered by the waist-high steel barriers lining the track, the occasional glimpse of the top of a car being no compensation for the shattering din which it is creating.

For the same price (approximately £25,000) it is possible to rent a top floor for the week in an apartment block overlooking the harbour and the circuit, but with enough capacity to seat 40 people for lunch under sun awnings on the roof. Williams arranged to have their sponsors use three floors of the apartment block positioned next to the Royal Box. On the fifteenth level, bottles of '93 Côtes de Provence were waiting on the linen tablecloths as the buffet was prepared and the guests took in the stunning view from the balcony running across the front of the apartment.

The entire lower portion of the track – from the exit of the tunnel, around the harbour, back along the start/finish straight and up the hill to the Hôtel de Paris and Casino Square – could be seen. A giant television screen on the rock face to the left took care of the sections of track which were out of sight. For the first-time visitor – indeed, for experienced hands at Monaco – this was a truly memorable way to watch a motor race and support 'your' team.

The only drawback from West's point of view was the fact that the comparatively inaccessible location meant the drivers would be unable to pay a flying visit in the limited time available on race morning. It was left to West to act as Williams representative, a role he played to perfection.

After bidding welcome on behalf of Rothmans Williams-Renault, West went into background detail on the team, revealing snippets about how 90 per cent of the parts used to build the cars were actually manufactured in-house by a team of more than 200 at Didcot. On hearing this there were looks of surprise from those members of the audience who believed the 20 or so mechanics seen on television executing pit stops were the sum total of the team. You could almost read their thoughts: 'They actually *make* the car as well!'

West got into his stride, describing the briefing sessions currently taking place as the drivers and engineers debated pit stop tactics and the set-up on the cars for the race. West had to somehow get over the fact that Damon Hill was on pole and yet, rather mysteriously, he had only been sixth-fastest in the warm-up. 'Trying something for the race which was not very successful,' was the inside line on that one. If only the answer would turn out to be so simple.

'Anyway,' said West, 'you're looking down on Ste-Dévote, the first corner. It's crucial to get a good start because overtaking is very difficult at Monaco. This time last year, I talked about Ste-Dévote and its importance. Damon went on to have a collision there and his race was over within minutes. I'm not saying anything this year!'

West's tact would make little difference. The assembled company had a fine aerial view of one Williams making a clean getaway and the other doing a balletic pirouette in the air after being squeezed by a Ferrari on either side. It was to be the start of a disappointing afternoon for everyone at Rothmans Williams-Renault, particularly Damon Hill, who was certain he would win.

Hill had been brilliant during qualifying, his car clearly at one with the track. Whereas others took the breath away as they entertained risk by urging recalcitrant machinery close to the barriers in search of that extra tenth of a second, Hill was the model of efficient speed and serenity, the Williams never once out of line. When he claimed pole position by almost a second, the race was as good as his.

Trouble had started during the warm-up on race morning. For some unaccountable reason, the Williams had become difficult to drive. At each of the many slow corners, the car wanted to understeer – go straight on – rather than tuck in neatly to the kerb or the barrier, as it had done during qualifying. No obvious solution could be found and hopes were not high as Hill went to the grid, directly below the three floors of guests who were blissfully unaware of the torment in the mind of their lead driver. But at least if Hill could get a good start, he would be able to dictate the pace.

Damon made a good getaway all right. But so too did Jean Alesi from a position directly behind Coulthard's Williams on the second row. As Alesi tried to squeeze through a narrowing gap on Coulthard's right, the Scotsman found himself in a Ferrari sandwich as Gerhard Berger forced his way through on the left. The pin-ball effect of the Williams bouncing between the two red cars had him spinning through the air before crash-landing back onto the track ahead of the Ferrari drivers, both of whom then tangled with each other for good measure.

The race was stopped, allowing Coulthard to abandon his badly damaged car and sprint back to the pits in time to take over the spare Williams for the re-start. This car was ear-marked for Hill and the mechanics barely had time to fit Coulthard's seat and adjust the pedals. At least this turn of events had given the overhead audience the bonus of a second start – although Hill probably did not share their pleasure as he contemplated having to beat Schumacher's Benetton all over again when they sprinted off the front row towards Ste-Dévote.

Hill managed it a second time but it would be the end of his pleasure that afternoon. The car felt no better and it was a struggle to pull away from the Benetton. Hill was planning to stop twice for fuel and tyres and he fervently hoped Schumacher would be doing the same. If not, then Williams were beaten because the Benetton could keep up while carrying more fuel.

Hill made his stop on schedule at the end of lap 23. The Williams crew anxiously waited for Schumacher to follow suit. Round and round he went, extending his lead, going faster than ever now that he had a clear track. Hill's problems, meanwhile, had been compounded by rejoining in the thick of back-markers. When Schumacher failed to stop after half a dozen laps or so, Hill knew the game was up.

Coulthard, meanwhile, was already out. In the race to prepare the spare car, there had not been enough time to properly calibrate the electronic control on the throttle. (Williams, in common with most leading teams, operated a 'fly-by-wire' throttle involving electronic sensors rather than a cable connecting the pedal to the hardware on the engine.) Coulthard found that, when he pressed the throttle pedal, first there was be no response at all – then suddenly full throttle. The telemetry would later show that he was experiencing wheel spin in every gear for up to 40 per cent of each lap; not the sort of thing a driver wants to have when confronted by walls, kerbs and steel barriers.

Nonetheless, Coulthard found he could adapt his driving to suit. Not so the gearbox, the dog rings inside eventually crying *Enough!* as the semi-automatic shift kept forcing them into action while the engine was revving much higher than normal. After 16 laps of this unavoidable abuse, the gearbox broke.

Disappointment high above in the sponsors' gallery was balanced by the thought that at least the other blue and white car was holding a commendable second place. It was perhaps just as well that the Rothmans guests could not read the thoughts of their driver. Frustrated would not even start to describe it. It became a very long afternoon for Damon as he worked his way through 78 laps of switch-back struggle.

When Hill trickled to a halt directly beneath the team's guests and climbed out to meet Prince Rainier, the sight of Schumacher punching the air made Hill's blood boil. Somehow, it had all gone wrong. Okay, second place at Monaco; very nice; thanks very much. But this was a race Hill wanted to win. And, by rights, he should have done so.

A picture of despair at the press conference, Hill brought his grievances with him to the Williams motor-home down by the harbour. There were no obvious answers why the car had understeered the way it did. And it seemed, with hindsight, that a one-stop strategy might have helped. Hill and the team had been convinced a single stop would be the way to go but the understeer problem during the warm-up threw them completely and it was decided to revert to two stops and a lighter fuel load in a bid to try and improve the handling. Once again, Williams appeared to have been totally eclipsed by Benetton.

When the truck drivers rolled into Didcot the following evening, the cars were quickly unloaded and stripped down. There was no time to lose since the team had to be ready to ship everything to Heathrow five days later in preparation for the flight to the Canadian Grand Prix.

In the midst of the hectic preparations came good news – of a sort. It was discovered that the differential fitted to Hill's car for race day at Monaco had been faulty. Since the differential governed the speed of the inside wheel relative to the much quicker outer wheel when negotiating a tight corner, it had an important part to play in Monte Carlo. But, with the differential more or less locked, the tendency would be for the car to understeer – or plough straight on. At least it answered one or two leading questions. But that was no consolation to Damon Hill as he mulled over a lost opportunity to retake the lead of the championship. As things stood, he was now trailing Schumacher by five points.

Still, at least the French salesforce from Rothmans – guests at Monaco – had applied themselves with renewed vigour when visiting shopkeepers who see perhaps 20 tobacco salesmen each week. Conversation would not have been a problem after their experience of the Williams-Renault team; barriers were broken down more easily.

'Damon Hill? Yes, met him, actually. Seems like a nice sort of chap; not bad for an Englishman! This is his second season driving for us. It's a great team, Rothmans Williams-Renault – which reminds me, we have this special promotion coming up for the French Grand Prix on 2 July . . .'

But, first, the sixth round of the championship in Montreal and the next phase of working through the team's budget. Williams, in keeping with most teams, do not reveal details of expenditure, but it can be assumed that it is at least £25m for the season – and that's without having to pay for engines. The majority of the team's income comes from sponsorship, expenditure going mainly on salaries and research and development.

Travel and transport accounts for at least £2m as the team clocks up 100,000 miles each year. When compared with other 'fly-away' races, the trip to Canada is short and relatively simple. It is also one of the most popular, the city of Montreal offering a splendid location for, shall we say, off-duty activities of various shapes and forms.

Certainly, the French influence provides numerous restaurants and David Coulthard took the opportunity to entertain the British press over an informal dinner on the night before practice began. This had no connection with sponsorship; just a shrewd piece of PR by the Scotsman, the return on his investment being a better understanding on all sides.

Coulthard had lent his name to the Savane fashion company, a direct endorsement which was used as part of a regular double-page Fantasy Grand Prix feature in

Autosport. This was a much more satisfactory method of advertising for Savane than the hugely expensive route of having identification on the car. It had taken seven weeks to put the programme together, clever background work by Coulthard and West leading to *Autosport* also carrying a Coulthard feature, published the week before Monaco.

The only thing missing, of course, was a consistent spread of results for David; the Monaco failure added to growing concern over Williams' reliability as the season marched past the first third. It didn't seem that things could get much worse. But they did.

The most unexpected source of trouble had come not long after the team had arrived in Montreal. Snatching a rare moment of relaxation, the mechanics had been playing in the hotel swimming pool when Gary Woodward, Number 1 on Coulthard's car, suffered a crushed disc in his back. Woodward was rushed to hospital and, just as quickly, a replacement mechanic was flown from England. This was the second set-back for Dickie Stanford on the personnel front, Steve Coates having been forced to miss the Canadian trip when he developed fluid on the lung shortly after Monaco. The sponsors, however, would not be interested in such personal minutiae. Their aim would be to see a return on their investment and Richard

West and his team would be on hand to ensure that they got it.

Canada was a more manageable venue for entertaining sponsors than Monte Carlo because the Paddock Club is located directly above the pits. Iain Cunningham and Victoria King of the marketing team would be at the sharp end of the operation, meeting and greeting and making sure that all reasonable requests were met.

Once again, race day would be the busiest – although not in terms of numbers since only eighty guests from Rothmans Ltd. (Canada), Black Tower, Sanyo and Segafredo would be present, albeit at £575 per head. Not surprisingly, value for money would be high on the agenda for the list of Williams sponsors, as they ensured their guests were adequately looked after.

But what about the team itself? Hill had been putting a brave face on the discovery of the differential problem in Monaco but, deep down, he was perplexed by the thought that the championship seemed to be slipping away by gradual degrees. After such a promising start to the season – when the Williams was superior to the Benetton – Williams had marked time, whereas Benetton had moved forward.

And so, too, had Ferrari. Schumacher was on pole in Canada with Hill alongside in second place – a reversal of Monaco – and it took an excellent effort by Coulthard during final qualifying to move ahead of the red cars and take third place. On top of all this, Hill had a head cold and his mood was not helped on race morning when he drew back his bedroom curtains in the smoked-glass Radisson Hotel to find the city skyline cloaked in grey cloud and rain.

The miserable conditions persisted throughout the morning warm-up and Hill was definitely no happier when he could only manage sixteenth fastest time. Coulthard was twelfth. Alesi was quickest, Berger third and Schumacher fourth. Worse than that, Hill had experienced gearbox problems with his race car. When he transferred to the spare car, a sticking throttle sent him into the gravel trap where he became stuck fast. His mood was not light, to say the least.

West and his team braced themselves. Hill and Coulthard were due to address the Paddock Club guests. It had to be hoped the drivers would not bring their troubles with them.

First, though, all 24 drivers would attend the official briefing at the far end of the paddock. After that, they would be free to eat, rest, discuss tactics further with their engineers or attend official functions. West usually earmarked the period immediately after the briefing, before the drivers got settled into anything else, but on this occasion it would be a seat-of-the-pants operation as

West took care not to have his drivers clash with rival operations next door.

The Paddock Club being a vast enclosure, each sponsor's area separated from the next by nothing more than a waist-high fence and pot plants, a booming voice from any loudspeaker could serve the company next door as well as the intended audience. Not long after the drivers' briefing had finished, the voice of Mark Blundell could be heard wafting from the Paddock Club, the McLaren enclosure being directly above the Williams garage. West went upstairs to survey the scene, reporting back by radio to Iain Cunningham that the driver addresses on either side of the Rothmans enclosures were about to wind down and could he have Hill and Coulthard on standby?

Damon was in the office and ready at a moment's notice. But David was nowhere to be seen. Reports filtered through that he had been stopped on his return from the drivers' briefing and was in deep discussion with Jackie Stewart. Cunningham, having worked for the former World Champion, knew exactly what that meant. The conversation, probably one-sided, was likely to go on for some time, particularly as Coulthard was a fellow Scot and had driven for Stewart's team in the junior formulas. Jackie, with the very best of intentions, was never slow to give excellent advice to his protégés. The only problem was such a conversation tended to be a lengthy one.

West, meanwhile, had given a five-minute countdown to Cunningham before starting his introduction. Two minutes to go and still no sign of Coulthard. Reports now indicated that he had finally got to his intended destination, the loo.

Five minutes came and went. West's powers of loquaciousness were being tested as Coulthard returned. Hill was summoned and, as Cunningham turned to leave, he was horrified to see Damon sidetracked by – Jackie Stewart. There was nothing for it but to politely interject, since West would soon burst into song and start taking requests if this continued.

Rather than take the recognized route via a staircase at the side of the pit buildings, Cunningham had devised a short-cut through the kitchens located in temporary Portacabins stacked one on top of the other at the back of the pits. Hill and Coulthard, in their blue and white driving overalls, jogged quickly up the narrow staircase and weaved past a hundred or more plates of prawn cocktail stacked neatly on dispensers and awaiting delivery to the tables. The smell, on this humid, overcast morning, was almost overpowering. Emerging onto the back terrace, the drivers turned right and walked the few yards to the Rothmans enclosure where West, deftly as you like, announced their arrival as if it had been planned to the split second.

It is a common failing of those permanently employed in Grand Prix racing to under-rate the power of a driver's presence when in the midst of his public. Occasions such as this serve as a sharp reminder. There was an audible increase in the buzz of anticipation, then a dip into silence, followed by enthusiastic applause. 'Their' drivers had come to visit.

Arranged in front of a large Rothmans backdrop, Coulthard and Hill engaged in a brief question and answer session with West before taking it in turn to describe a lap of the circuit. After signing the circuit map and posing briefly for photographs, Hill – in surprisingly good form – and Coulthard bade farewell and walked next door to the Renault enclosure, where they went through the same procedure with another circuit map for the benefit of guests from the Renault's North American subsidiary, Mack Trucks. Then it was a swift escape through the mountain of prawn cocktails and down the stairs to the paddock.

The Rothmans enclosure was abuzz for quite some time, guests eyeing the signed circuit map which would later be the star prize in a raffle. In the background, white-hatted chefs presided over 15 simmering silver salvers laden with food. The circular tables were set for lunch, each place having a gift of a disposable camera in blue and white with stickers suitably in place to match the Rothmans Canadian symbols.

The best pictures of the day would undoubtedly come from the front balcony, overhead the Benetton garage with the Williams pit placed nicely to the right. Having met the drivers and about to dine in comfort – as opposed to the paying public wallowing in the muddy enclosure opposite and making do with hamburgers – the guests were set for a first-class race. Would the Rothmans Williams-Renault team be in a position to reciprocate?

Hill had been upbeat in public but, privately, he was not so sure. The rain had stopped but, unlike Imola, the track was dry enough to warrant starting on slick tyres. Either way – wet or dry – Hill was not very confident in the handling of the car.

There was also the question of pit stops. The pit lane entry was actually quite short and the exit fast, allowing for very little time loss when stopping to change tyres and take on fuel. But, set against that, the tight nature of the circuit and the numerous chicanes meant overtaking would be very difficult. It would therefore be virtually impossible to make up time in event of more than one pit stop. Another important variable would be the high fuel consumption induced by this circuit. Just one stop would make the tank capacity very marginal on the run to the flag. Williams were to wish they had the luxury of getting that far.

David Coulthard's grandparents had flown to Canada for the race. They were seated in the main grandstand opposite the pits. Their grandson passed them just once at speed. On the second lap, while defending third place from the squabbling Ferraris, Coulthard lost control on a damp patch and one of the many bumps characterizing the circuit. He had been braking hard for one of the chicanes when the car snapped sideways with a violence which was impossible to counteract. Somehow the Ferraris missed him but the damage was done when the Williams slithered into the gravel trap. Coulthard was left to contemplate his third race in succession without any points.

Hill was only marginally better off. Schumacher was pulling away and the Williams driver could offer no resistance as first Alesi and then Berger slipped through. Hill's luck began to turn when Berger ran out of fuel as he made his way towards the pit lane and his one and only stop. By the time he had free-wheeled in, taken on fuel and got going again, the Ferrari was out of the leading equation.

Hill was third and, under the circumstances, reasonably content to be there. Then, to his disbelief, the car became stuck in gear and the engine died. The hydraulic pump had failed – an exact repeat of the last lap in Spain. The only difference this time was that the total shutdown happened immediately. And he came to a halt right under the noses of his pit crew.

Hill was speechless with rage. He literally burst from the cockpit, wrenching himself free from the radio and drink lines attached to his crash helmet. The Rothmans guests had the perfect view of their man erupting from the far side of the pit wall before climbing over and landing heavily in the pit lane. Almost tearing his fingers off with the blue flameproof gloves, Hill marched into the garage and delivered a brief but vituperative speech to Frank Williams. Then he stormed through the back door, hurled himself into the office, where he quickly got changed. By the time he had dressed, the British media was gathered by the door. What Hill had to say in haste would make mean headlines the following day. With hardly a goodbye, he gathered his things and headed for the car park.

Having reached his hotel, Hill had become more circumspect. Aware of the possible damage his earlier remarks might cause, he began to set things right by dictating his post-race column in a more reflective manner, saying he was not apportioning blame, that they had to work as a team to pull themselves back to their rightful position.

A phone call to the circuit ascertained that Alesi had

won his first Grand Prix in ninety-one attempts. So what had become of Schumacher? Gearbox trouble had brought the Benetton into the pits where repairs soon had Schumacher rejoining in seventh place. But, as luck would have it, Berger contrived to crash into Martin Brundle's Ligier, taking them both out as they disputed fifth place – and suddenly Schumacher was on course for two points.

Once again, however, the sponsors had enjoyed their day. The final snacks and glasses of wine were consumed in the Paddock Club while, down below, the team quietly and efficiently went about their packing. Paul Edwards began to clear the kitchen, removing beer from the fridge and passing it out to willing hands in the garage. Then he studied a bottle of champagne for a second or two. Like those diverse dinners in Monaco two weeks before, it was a question of knowing exactly how to handle each occasion. He gave the bottle a gentle pat and placed it back in the box. Hopefully it would be put to good use at the end of the next round in France.

CHAPTER FOUR

POWER AND PRINT

FRANCE AND BRITAIN

It was like some abandoned ship. The Renault motor-home was empty, the pine tables under the white awning vacant for perhaps the first time during the Silverstone weekend. Or, at least, *this* particular Renault enclave – the one opposite the Williams motor-home – was totally deserted.

Not ten yards away, Renault's other base was a swirling mass of humanity as revellers from the Benetton bus spilled into the French quarter to drink their champagne and celebrate victory for Johnny Herbert.

This was the divide between winning and losing, with Renault – engine supplier to both teams – stuck uncomfortably in the middle. And what made it worse was the fact that Michael Schumacher and Damon Hill, representing Benetton and Williams respectively, had collided while disputing the lead. Renault did not know which way to turn.

At least Herbert, by winning his first Grand Prix under ecstatic circumstances at home, had saved the day. Jean Alesi's Ferrari had been poised to pick up the pieces and success for the Italian marque in such an important market-place would have been too much for Renault to take. By supporting two of the top teams with what was considered to be the best engine, Renault expected nothing less than victory.

Renault had been racing with Williams since the beginning of the 1989 season but their Grand Prix history went back much further than that. Right back, in fact, to the dusty, pioneering days of the sport itself when Louis and Marcel Renault, founders of the marque, took their own cars to victory in events such as the Paris–Ostend in 1899. Renault's proud heritage meant very little, however, when they entered contemporary Grand Prix racing in 1977. The first appearance of the yellow and white car at Silverstone was something of a novelty since the engine was turbocharged, Renault being the first manufacturer to explore this loophole in the regulations.

The V6 turbo may have lasted no more than 17 laps that day but the writing was on the paddock wall for those who cared to read it. Seven years later, all but a handful of runners would be powered by a turbocharged engine, although Renault failed to capitalize on their advantage and never won the championship before turbos were finally banned at the end of 1988.

Liaison with Lotus and other teams had made it clear that the task of building both the engine and the car was too much to take on. It was better to be an engine supplier rather than a fully-blown entrant tackling every single aspect of a hugely complex business. After a brief hiatus, Renault decided to do the job properly in 1989, this time by concentrating on what they knew best and by leaving the design of the car and the running of the team to Williams Grand Prix Engineering. In 1992, Nigel Mansell gave the Paris-based company their first world title at the wheel of a Williams-Renault.

By the time of the 1995 Canadian Grand Prix, Renault had scored their hundredth pole position and sixty-second victory. The only problem, as far as Williams were concerned, was the fact that the Renault V10 had been in the back of a Benetton in each case for each of these landmark results. Just to rub it in, a gushing press release from Benetton praised Renault to the sky and ever so graciously offered to carry the Renault name on the rear wing as a mark of respect. The fact that the space was usually occupied by identification for sponsor Mild

Seven – but not allowed in Canada because of anti-tobacco legislation – was a handy coincidence.

Nonetheless, such ingratiating behaviour was deliberately employed by Benetton since it flew in the face of the more traditional and stiff upper lip practices employed by Williams. It exacerbated the discomfort felt by Williams ever since Renault had revealed their intention to supply Benetton in 1995.

Previously, Renault had powered Ligier, a second-division team receiving second-preference treatment from the engine manufacturer. Williams could live with that. But Benetton? This was something else. Benetton would, quite rightly, demand equal status. And Renault would provide it with unquestioned impartiality. There could be no complaints on that score but the simmering discontent within Williams spilled onto the pages of *Autosport* in the issue published a few days before the British Grand Prix.

Patrick Head, using the no-nonsense attitude which had become his hallmark, made clear his reservations. 'We were not happy about Renault supplying engines to Benetton,' said Head. 'We told them that last year [1994] and they said they were going to do it anyway. They were free individuals but they knew our point of view and they made their decision. We weren't happy about it then and we're not happy about it now.' With further words to that effect, Head made it clear that Williams were not prepared to put up with such an arrangement in the long term. His words were not well received by Renault.

On the Thursday night before the British Grand Prix weekend, Michel Gigou, managing director of Renault UK, hosted a dinner party for the British press at the Bricklayer's Arms in the Warwickshire village of Priors Hardwick. Present were Patrick Faure, the head of Renault Sport, and Bernard Dudot, the brilliant engineer who is affectionately known as 'the father' of the Renault V10.

Dudot looked tired. These had been a very busy few weeks, a period of constant pressure given that the French and the British Grands Prix – the most important for Renault and Williams – were two weeks apart. Renault had applied further pressure on themselves by introducing the latest evolution of their engine for the French race, a traditional time on home turf to unveil the next stage in the search for increased performance.

This year, however, there had been twice the amount of work since Renault were supplying two top teams. Apart from making sure that the latest engine was reliable, Dudot had to build twenty of them (ten for each team for France), ensure spare parts were on stream and then continue the production run for the rest of the season. It was commitment of the highest magnitude. If one engine failed in this increasingly intense battle between Williams and Benetton, Dudot's name would be mud. Small wonder he looked weary that night.

The last thing he needed was questions about Head's comments in the press. Dudot, in fact, held Patrick in very high regard. They were pragmatic and talented engineers who spoke the same language and understood each other's needs – a compromise frequently absent in the essential make-up of the relationship between the engine and car manufacturers. If anything, Dudot could probably sympathize with Head's stance over the business of engine-sharing. But politics were not Bernard's game. He would leave the answers to Patrick Faure.

'Do you think, in the light of Patrick Head's comments, that the relationship with Williams is about to end?' Faure was asked.

'No,' he replied immediately. 'Patrick is the engineer. It is Frank who makes these decisions and I am sure we will continue. It is a very good relationship.'

Reading between the lines of such a polite put-down, it was clear that Faure was still simmering over the content of the interview. Even so, there was no mistaking that Head had made his point. Now, of course, Williams would have to back that up at Silverstone by avenging the punishment delivered two weeks earlier in France. It was Benetton which had delivered the goods on Renault's home ground, in front of an influential audience.

Renault had brought 6,000 to the race at Magny-Cours, their yellow caps peppering the grandstands running the length of the pit straight. These were employees from the factories and dealers and their clients. The tickets were not entirely free but Renault had paid the lion's share and given each guest a bag of goodies, including T-shirt, cap, ear plugs, programme and a map of the circuit. The VIP Club catered for 350 guests at $1,000 a head while, in the Renault hospitality box, the company chairman and chief executive, Louis Schweitzer, held court on race day.

As official supplier for the French Grand Prix, Renault had provided 150 vehicles, ranging from the executive Safrane for the race organizer to transport for the stewards and doctors, shuttles for the photographers and a high-performance Clio Maxi to act as 'Safety Car'. Such an outlay brought huge headaches, not the least being the need to find an additional forty passes to allow the various mechanics, drivers and chauffeurs to ensure the smooth running of the transport programme.

Such mundane matters were of no interest to Bernard Dudot as his latest brainchild was run in public for the first time. In broad terms, the Renault RS7B did not provide an increase in power over the RS7 but, rather, subtle improvements to the performance across the range, from the torque propelling the car out of slow corners to maximum effort at full revs on the straight.

■■

In Dudot's parlance, the engine was more 'driveable' in all situations. In other words, it would make it easier for the driver to extract the best from the car and engine throughout the 2.6-mile lap. Tests had shown this to be the case; Dudot knew it worked; practice had proved it as Renault-powered cars filled the first three places on the grid, with Hill starting from pole and Schumacher alongside. So far so good.

But the worry remained. Could Dudot's baby cope with the stresses of a 190-mile race? For an hour and 40 minutes, the ten pistons in each engine would endure constant periods of maximum acceleration measuring approximately 8,000g. The peak loading on the connecting rod would be three tons. If the piston was released from the cylinder as it accelerated from rest to maximum speed in one thousandth of a second, there would be enough energy to fling it more than 300 feet into the air. That sort of explosive force had to be contained within the aluminium cylinder block and head. Dudot probably didn't care to think about it as he walked to the rear of the Williams garage.

Donning his head-set and pulling out a small stool, he sat down in front of a bank of screens and waited for the truth to emerge in minute detail. From here on, he would be riding in the cars with Damon and David; in fact, he would know more about what was going on in the engines

■■

than the drivers themselves, thanks to the wonder of telemetry.

'An engineer without telemetry is as blind as a doctor without a stethoscope,' said Dudot. 'It has been a revolution in our world. Telemetry is a remote X-ray of an engine, done by continuous analysis of the essential parameters: a photograph of its behaviour. It is an area in which Renault did the pioneering work.

'In 1985 we first installed an on-board black box on Ayrton Senna's Lotus-Renault. At the time, data was not transmitted by radio, so we had to wait until the car stopped in the pits before plugging in a portable computer and emptying the black box of its vital information. We can now interpret what is happening inside the engine without the car having to stop in the pits. We have a continuous flow of data which can be processed instantaneously.'

As the French Grand Prix screamed relentlessly by on the track not a hundred metres from Dudot's back, his picture of events was being defined by oil and fuel pressures, oil and water temperatures, engine revs, fuel consumption, gear selection, the speed of the cars, lap times and overall positions in the race. All this was being relayed by a kaleidoscope of blipping cursors, rapidly changing numerals and intricate graphics. The translation into hard fact said that the Renault RS7Bs in the back of the Williams and Benettons were running faultlessly. Hill was leading, with Schumacher hard on his tail. Coulthard was third.

At the end of lap 19, Schumacher dived into the pits for his first routine stop. Having seen the signal on Schumacher's pit board, Hill had got on the radio and asked to do exactly the same. He was told that Coulthard was on his way in. In the next two laps, as Hill struggled through a clutch of back-markers, he lost seven seconds. By the time he shot into the pits for his fuel and tyres at the end of lap 21, Schumacher was into a lead he would never lose. Worse than that, he was pulling away by half a second a lap. Hill was helpless.

But at least Renault were happy since the cast of 6,000 was witnessing their engines powering home the first three. The actual politics behind the scenes was of no interest to them. Williams had been beaten, pure and simple. But, as the information was recorded and stored on Dudot's computer, the bottom line was that all three RS7B engines had performed perfectly. The fourth, in the Benetton of Johnny Herbert, had run for just two laps before the Englishman was forced into a spin by Jean Alesi's Ferrari. Such a retirement, while being disappointing, was of little concern to the Renault technicians.

For Williams, however, this had been a disaster by their high standards – but nowhere near as bad as Canada three weeks earlier. At least Hill had won pole and the cars had been reliable. That much was a step forward. Even so, Schumacher had extended his lead of the championship to 11 points – not the end of the world, but a disappointment nonetheless.

Hill was mulling this over as he waited in the warm, still air of early evening for Frank Williams's jet to be prepared for the flight to England. A familiar figure crossed the tarmac. 'I know that face,' thought Hill. 'Who is he?'

'I just wanted to say that I thought you did a fantastic job today,' said the man, clearly an enthusiast who had watched the race. It was only then that Damon realized he was shaking hands with Placido Domingo, just about the last person he expected to find on a small airfield in the middle of France. It was a timely intervention, the opera singer's genuine good wishes reminding Hill that leading a race and finishing second was not so bad after all. Even so, as Damon boarded the plane, along with his engineer, David Brown, and Adrian Newey, designer of the Williams, there was only one thing on everyone's mind: setting the record straight at Silverstone in a fortnight's time.

Such things were not to the forefront in the thoughts of the team in the Williams minibuses heading to the airport at Clermont-Ferrand. With the chartered Air 2000 Boeing 757 unable to land at Nevers, the team had no

■ ■

alternative but to flog south for an hour and a half; not what they needed at end of a typically arduous weekend.

Dickie Stanford's task had not been made easy by the discovery on Friday of cracks in the spokes of one set of their Italian-made wheels. It was noted that the Jordan team, who used the same supplier, had unexpectedly experienced cracks in their wheels during the Monaco Grand Prix weekend. Williams did not take any chances but the precautionary measure meant four men had been tied up checking between 20 and 24 sets of wheels after each practice session. In the end, nothing had been found. But the consequences of a broken wheel in the middle of a 150-m.p.h. corner did not bear thinking about.

As the mechanics shoved their brown tweed jackets into the overhead racks and flopped into the seats of the 757, they did not want to contemplate what, for most, would be the worst weekend of the year: their home Grand Prix. One would think it would be the opposite: no airports, foreign languages or ambivalent crowds supporting some other team; a race to enjoy in front of an appreciative audience. While all that may be true, the pressures and expectations of performing at home are huge. Williams had won the British Grand Prix for the previous four years; friends and casual observers would automatically assume that a fifth victory was there for the taking.

■ ■

And, of course, they would want to visit Silverstone and see it happen. Easier said than done on every count.

With the majority of teams based in Britain – and most within a quick drive from Silverstone – paddock passes, already strictly limited, were impossible to find. It was difficult to explain such a thing to factory staff who had worked above and beyond the call of duty in order to allow the team to go racing in the first place. It seemed reasonable to expect to be able to see the product of their labour in action.

Mind you, it was also reasonable to expect the race mechanics to be able to go about their business without the garages and pit lane being full of idle hands. It was a dilemma team managers such as Dickie Stanford had to resolve – with the greatest tact – along with all their other tasks. The priority was to get the job done and, by Saturday evening, Williams-Renault were halfway there; Damon Hill was on pole with David Coulthard starting from the second row, directly behind his team-mate. In between them, the inevitable presence of Michael Schumacher and Benetton-Renault. It was exactly the high-pressure situation which the nation had come to expect, thanks to a week of unprecedented hype by the media.

If you believed everything you read, Hill and Schumacher were at each others' throats and UN peace-keeping troops were about to be drafted into the paddock. In fact, various quotes had been taken out of context, particularly one which Hill had given in an interview eight months earlier. Referring to the strict schooling for young drivers implemented by the Mercedes-Benz sports car team at the turn of the decade, Hill had been commenting on the fact that such methods, for all their undoubted value, tended to produce stereotyped drivers. He cited Michael Schumacher as an example. Unfortunately, he also used the word 'clone', in its broadest sense. Sadly, that was translated into German as 'clown'. Then it was claimed that Hill had just said it, out of the blue, a week before Silverstone. Major wars have been started for less.

Hill defused the situation as best he could at a press conference in a tent at the back of the paddock. Such matters were of no importance in the garages as Dickie Stanford stood, hands on hips, surveying the four racing cars parked before him. Normally, the team only brought one spare car. But, because this was Silverstone and in close proximity to the team headquarters, a second back-up car was brought along – one for each driver. Trouble was, the decision had been made late in the week and now the team manager was trying to accommodate the extra mechanics involved. Some of the lads would have to sleep three to a room in the team's hotel in nearby Buckingham. It was a less than ideal solution.

Meanwhile, copies of *Autosport* were being examined

in the Renault motor-home parked across the way from the royal-blue Williams bus. The pages containing Patrick Head's trenchant interview would be well thumbed come Saturday evening.

The mood was light in the Williams compound that night, thanks to Hill's second pole position in succession. Happily for the team, they had chosen Saturday evening to host a curry party for members of the press. The supply of Labatts 'Ice' beer was under immediate attack at the end of an overcast and humid day interspersed with heavy rain showers. By 8 p.m., Hilary Weaver, the chef who worked with Paul Edwards and his wife, Frances, was sending the smell of spice wafting across the paddock as the hungry hacks formed a reasonably orderly queue.

Perhaps sensing discomfort in the French quarter across the way, Patrick Head was in a truculent mood as he came away from the final debrief with Adrian Newey and his engineers, David Brown and Jock Clear. Removing his team uniform in the motor-home, Head donned denim jeans and a leather jacket, picked up a crash helmet and descended into the temporary dining room spread outside the bus. As he stopped at various tables to make colourful remarks to the media, the subject of his interview quickly entered the conversation.

'Patrick Faure says you're just the engineer and, in any case, it's Frank who makes the important decisions,' said

■ ■

one journalist, feigning innocence and obviously trying to be helpful. Head smiled, refused to rise to the bait cast by this touch of artistic licence, bade his farewell and went to find his traffic-beating Yamaha XJ900 motorcycle.

David Coulthard, having dined on pasta and barbecued chicken with Renault, headed off to the Towcester Cycling Club to visit members of his fan club. Damon Hill, having called in on his relatives, staying overnight in a caravan parked on the infield camp side, returned to the Williams motor-home and received a rowdy reception from the fans waiting patiently by the paddock fence. Starved of autographs and limited to only the briefest glimpse of their hero as he ducked in and out of the motor-home, Hill's supporters sensed that the moment was right.

Hill was only to happy to oblige – even to the extent of finding a decent marker pen before walking to the fence and climbing onto an oil drum, the better to receive the proffered programmes and scraps of paper as they were poked through the fence. One fan became so excited that he dialled his girlfriend and passed the mobile phone over the wire for Damon to have a word. The girlfriend, not believing who she was speaking to, became distinctly uneasy when informed that her boyfriend seemed to be having a great time, surrounded by beautiful women and bottles of beer. The conversation was swiftly terminated.

When the signing and chatting had been completed,

■ ■

Damon returned to the motor-home and phoned his wife, Georgie, expecting their third child any day. They discussed the possibility of Georgie flying from Dublin to Silverstone by private plane (no commercial airline would accept a woman in such an advanced stage of pregnancy), provided the doctor gave the all-clear. Damon would later explain that Georgie worried more when she was not at the race track, although it was easy to sense the fact that he needed the company. He was not exactly feeling a warm embrace from his team even though that was partly a situation of his own making.

Patrick Head and Frank Williams had not taken kindly to Damon's criticism of their car and their tactics in the immediate aftermath of recent races. That was understandable to a degree, the team chiefs having experienced many a harsh word as racing drivers, frustrated by failure, gave immediate vent to their feelings. But more difficult to accept had been a quote in that Thursday's edition of *The Times* when Damon's solicitor, Michael Breen, had uncharacteristically allowed his position of tactful silence to slip when he offered his opinion in print.

Discussing rumours which were running riot concerning Hill's plans for 1996, Breen said: 'Usually, everyone waits for the top one or two drivers to slot into their positions. Traditionally, decisions are made at Monza in September. This year it is going to be accelerated, partly because Schumacher has let it be known how much he is looking for. He has started the game much earlier than usual. Everyone has to turn their mind to dealing with his demands and work out whether they want him or not.'

Then Breen ventured into contentious territory. 'If they don't want him [Schumacher], the alternative is Damon. Damon's next deal will be a big one and the rules have changed a little bit for Williams. Benetton now have Renault engines, too, and the Benetton car is every bit as good a car – and Ferrari have also closed the gap significantly performance-wise. Williams can no longer say: "We are giving you head and shoulders the best car above all the other cars and therefore we do not need to pay you as much." '

That went down like a cup of cold sick. Williams did not like having their business dissected in the media in this manner and, besides, they had never claimed in 1994 that their car was head and shoulders above the rest. That accolade had gone to Benetton for the best part of the season. Indeed, if anything, the 1994 Williams-Renault had been difficult to drive and Hill had deserved his subsequent 1995 pay rise for that fact alone.

Doubtless Damon had felt the bristles as he arrived at Silverstone on the Thursday. Still, he had made amends by taking pole position with a brilliant lap, one which was brimful of aggression and determination.

As Hill ended his phone call to Dublin, he picked up the latest issue of *Autosport* and flicked through the Grand Prix preview. As he did so, something caught his eye on page 35. A highlighted quote said: 'At Monaco, even if we had gone for a one-stop strategy, I still think we would have finished second.'

Hill looked more closely. These were further words from Patrick Head in the same interview which had caused such offence at Renault. Now Head was saying that the differential trouble experienced by Hill at Monaco 'was a minor problem that almost certainly had no effect on the outcome of the race'.

Damon raised his eyes to the ceiling. Just what he wanted to read on the eve of the British Grand Prix! In an environment being wound very tight by the printed word, that made the score 1–1. But there was much worse to follow on Sunday afternoon.

With there being little to choose between the Benetton and the Williams, pit stop tactics would probably decide the outcome. It was a sensitive issue as far as Williams were concerned, one which Adrian Newey had addressed at a press conference earlier in the weekend. Answering questions about the apparent inability to bring Hill in at the right moment at Magny-Cours, Newey said:

....

'It is very easy to criticize race strategy afterwards. Firstly, at Magny-Cours it was suggested that we should have stopped earlier. But if we had brought Damon in earlier it would have run David out of fuel. Sometimes you get it wrong, and sometimes you get it right. It is difficult to be terribly scientific about it. You can come up with computer programs to try and predict this and that, but at the end of the day it is down to the humans on the pit wall trying to make decisions at the time.'

Nonetheless, the Williams team examined and discussed every possible angle as they sat in the debriefing room at the back of the truck. The best available information suggested there was very little to choose between one stop and two, in which case it would be preferable to make the most of the benefit which would come with having fresh tyres at a later stage on the race. Two stops seemed to be the way to go and, given a fair wind, they might just be ahead of Benetton when all the stops had been completed. They had certain facts before them: air temperature 21°C; track temperature 28°C; humidity 56 per cent and rising; rainfall zero; wind speed 9.4 k.p.h. from the south-west. But, as Newey said, it would largely be a seat-of-the-pants operation from the humans at the pit wall. This is what they saw on Sunday, 16 July 1995:

Hill makes a perfect start from pole position. Coulthard is just as quick from third place – but not fast enough to

....

■ ■

counter an incredible getaway by Jean Alesi as the Ferrari storms through from the third row. The good news, however, is that Alesi has slotted into second place – ahead of Schumacher.

Hill sees a red car in his mirror. 'Brilliant!' he thinks. 'Thank you! *Thank you!*' Hill makes the most of this bonus and takes the Williams to the limit, extending his lead by over a second each lap.

But where's Schumacher? Damon had expected the Benetton to pass the Ferrari sooner or later but, apparently, Michael is making no attempt to take second place. That can only mean one thing; the Benetton is heavy with fuel and is therefore making just one stop. Now Hill knows precisely what he has to do; keep driving flat out because this is going to be exceptionally close.

Hill is 18.3 seconds ahead as Alesi makes a scheduled stop at the end of lap 18. Now we'll see what Schumacher can do, given a clear track. He is knocking a second a lap off Hill but Damon sets his best lap so far before taking his turn in the pits.

Schumacher leads, but he is not making much headway, thanks to back-markers. His advantage over Hill is 9.7 seconds but the gap comes down to 7.8 seconds, then 7.6 seconds. Now Hill is struggling and Schumacher is clear. His lead extends to 9.3 seconds, then 10.0, 10.9, 11.4, 12.0, the Benetton now running as light as it will

■ ■

ever be as his one and only pit stop approaches at the end of lap 31.

Hill is back in front again, Schumacher 21.3 seconds behind. Hill, of course, has one more stop to come. Now the Williams is running lighter than the Benetton. Hill eases out the gap to 22.1 seconds, then 22.6. He sets his fastest lap of the race on lap 37; the gap is 25.0 seconds. Will that be enough? Hill took 40 seconds to get in and out of the pits first time round; Schumacher (taking on more fuel of course) was in for 43 seconds. Keep going! Keep going! Hill presses on, but it will not be enough.

Hill is in the pit lane for 40.5 seconds at the end of lap 41. Schumacher takes the lead.

Hill rejoins; the two cars should have more or less the same amount of fuel on board. But Hill has fresh tyres. And he has the Benetton in his sights. Within two laps, Hill is on Schumacher's tail. The 90,000 crowd goes berserk, the enclosures awash with Union flags. The Benetton is locking brakes; Schumacher is under huge pressure. At last! A fight to the finish between these two.

Not quite.

Coming towards the second-gear left-hander at Priory, Schumacher makes a wide approach on the right. Hill, travelling much faster – but coming from a long way back – goes for the gap on the inside. It may be his only chance before the benefit of fresh tyres is gone.

Schumacher begins to turn into the corner. But Hill has not come far enough to rightfully claim it as his. Yet he is completely committed. Realizing the gap is disappearing rapidly, Hill brakes even harder, his left front wheel sending a distress signal of blue rubber smoke as the brake pads lock onto the glowing disc brake and hold it firm. And still Schumacher keeps coming. The Williams smacks into the side of the Benetton. Both cars career onto the gravel and into retirement on the outside of the corner.

The moment has been caught on the giant television screens around the circuit. It is one of the extraordinary capacities of a racing driver that he can concentrate on hurtling through corners at 150 m.p.h. in close company and yet have the ability to glance at a screen and register in an instant the detail and significance of the picture.

'That's interesting!' thought David Coulthard as he caught a fleeting glimpse of his team-mate and Schumacher extricating themselves from the mess. Having been in fourth place (thanks to moving ahead of Alesi during the round of pit stops) and chasing Johnny Herbert's Benetton, Coulthard realized he had inherited second place – and was now challenging Herbert for the lead!

Not quite.

As he closed on the Benetton, the television screen once more became a messenger of doom and, this time,

Damon Hill rushes out of the pit lane at Brazil's Interlagos circuit.

Changing gear. The mechanics don their flameproof clothing in
the back of the garage in preparation for the refuelling stops during
the Brazilian Grand Prix.

Hands on. Dickie Stanford, the team manager, uses past experience as a mechanic to lend a hand during preparation in Argentina.

Visor up, eyes down. David Coulthard prepares to leave the pit lane for serious business on the track.

Powering onto the pit straight. Damon Hill heads for
victory at Imola.

Under wraps. Several sets of tyres cooking nicely in the paddock.
Steve Coates checks the temperatures as the electric blankets do their work.

Temporary hold-up. Dressed like bandits in their flamepro

ear, mechanics set to work during a pit stop at Imola.

Full lock at Loews. David Coulthard hauls his Williams round
the tight hairpin outside Monaco's Loews Hotel.

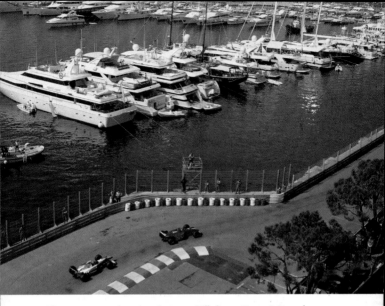

The most expensive game in town. Hill chases Berger's Ferrari onto the glittering harbour-front as Grand Prix racing makes its annual visit to Monaco.

Hill: a struggle into second place in France.

Fenced out. Damon Hill greets his fans at Silverstone.

Backward march. Photographers trip over themselves as they attempt to catch Michael Schumacher's grim expression as he returns to the Silverstone paddock on foot following the collision with Damon Hill.

■■■■■■■■■■■■■■■■■■■■■■■■■■■■■■■■■

the news was not in David's favour. Across the bottom of the picture, a blue graphic indicated that Coulthard would have to visit the pits for a ten-second stop-go penalty. The crime: speeding in the pit lane.

Coulthard was not unduly surprised. The electrics had failed on his car not long after the first pit stop. This had affected the semi-automatic gearchange and Coulthard had been waiting for the gearbox to fail. But, to his great surprise, it kept going, the only problem now being the fact that the electrical problem had also affected the speed-limiter which keeps the car at the required 120 k.p.h. (75 m.p.h.) in the pit lane.

On his second stop, Coulthard had to apply guesswork, a task as difficult as driving fast on a motorway and then immediately reducing speed for a 30 m.p.h. limit without having the benefit of a speedometer. David knew it would only be a matter of minutes before the team called him but, in the meantime, he was right with Herbert. So why not take the lead while the brief opportunity lasted?

In a neat piece of out-braking on lap 49 (aided, in part, by Herbert also being aware of his rival's penalty), Coulthard moved to the front of his home Grand Prix and stayed there for two laps. Then came the inevitable call.

By the time he had paid his penance, Coulthard was third, once more behind Alesi's Ferrari. Johnny Herbert would win his first Grand Prix to emotional scenes, a

■■■■■■■■■■■■■■■■■■■■■■■■■■■■■■■■■

victory which no one would begrudge the Essex driver, given the desperate trials and tribulations he had been forced to endure these past six years.

Williams had seen both their cars lead the British Grand Prix and all they had to show for it was one third place. Hill's welcome on his return to the garage had been – blunt. He was clearly being blamed for an accident which, in truth, was the unfortunate product of racing in the Nineties.

The race stewards apportioned blame equally and, by so doing, came close to admitting that the sport itself was at fault. The accident had been prompted by Grand Prix racing's most fundamental failing: the inability of one driver to overtake another without either risking an accident or relying completely on the charity of the man in front.

Thanks to the enormous amounts of downforce created by the cars – and in particular the front and rear wings – the braking distances are so short that the modern Formula One car can decelerate from 180 to 60 m.p.h. in less than two seconds and in the space of 120 yards. Attempting a passing move under such circumstances requires commitment and courtesy – that's assuming the second driver can get close enough to the one in front without the backwash of turbulent air seriously affecting the nose wings and therefore the handling of his car.

■■■■■■■■■■■■■■■■■■■■■■■■■■■■■■■■■■■■■

Such technical niceties were irrelevant three hours after the race had finished. As the Benetton mechanics took their time and savoured the moment, the Williams garage was completely clear of motor racing paraphernalia, every last banner and nut and bolt loaded onto the three trucks parked outside.

The vast area had become a temporary dining room as Paul Edwards wheeled in a barbecue and cooked supper for the mechanics and employees from the factory. With no chairs or tables available, they sat quietly on the concrete floor and rested against the grey breeze-block walls.

There was not a Renault person in sight.

■■■■■■■■■■■■■■■■■■■■■■■■■■■■■■■■■■■■■

CHAPTER FIVE

TELL ME
ABOUT IT

GERMANY AND HUNGARY

The car which had been assigned to Damon Hill for the German Grand Prix remained in a box throughout the weekend of the next race in Hungary. It had been stripped down and repaired. By consigning the chassis to a packing case, it was almost as if the team did not wish to be reminded about the debacle at Hockenheim.

The last time that car – chassis Number 4 – had appeared in public, it had been a sorry sight; the suspension arms bent, the bodywork battered, the once-gleaming paintwork covered in dust. A pick-up truck had visited the tyre wall lining the outer edge of the first corner, extricated the wreckage and dumped it outside the Williams garage, where it was trolleyed inside for the dismantling process to begin.

• •

Not far away, chassis Number 5 sat in the post-race scrutineering compound, its bodywork coated with a sticky mix of oil and rubber; a more acceptable anointment which said this car had completed the full race distance and finished in second place. But, in Williams parlance, that was not good enough. Not by a long way.

They had expected to win at Hockenheim. Second place was not much help on a day when Michael Schumacher had scored an emotional victory at home and extended his lead to 21 points. What made it worse was the fact that Damon Hill had scored none, for it was his car that sat forlornly on the garage floor.

Hill had started from pole. Schumacher and Benetton had been in trouble all weekend and Damon appeared to have it made. As he crossed the line at the end of the first lap, he was already 1.3 seconds ahead of the Benetton. But that's as far as it went. At the point where he would turn in to the first corner, a reasonably fast right-hander, the Williams went into a spin.

Hill was a passenger from then on as the car careered backwards across the gravel trap and deposited him into the tyre wall at the feet of several thousand baying Schumacher fans. Ignominious does not make a start on it in the catalogue of unscheduled departures. Hill couldn't explain it. The team was speechless.

Seven hours later, David Brown was shuffling through passport control at Heathrow's Terminal 1.

'I remember seeing Damon doing exactly the same thing, at exactly the same corner, in a Formula 3000 race,' piped a helpful soul.

'Tell me about it,' replied Brown, a wry smile emphasizing the sarcasm. Such historical niceties would do little either to repair the damage or answer the burning question of just why Hill had apparently chucked a weekend's work into the tyre wall. David Brown wanted to know the answer as much as, if not more than, anyone else.

As Hill's engineer, Brown shared every mechanical nuance, every technical detail and every tactical decision with his driver. They had just spent two days of practice, plus the race morning warm-up, perfecting the car.

They had dealt in millimetres and notches, fractional adjustments to tyre pressures, detailed examination of terminal speeds. They had dissected each lap into milliseconds, measured the time taken to enter and leave the pit lane, computed the race in theory, allowed for every variation, gone on gut feeling. As little as possible had been left to chance. And then the driver had tossed it all away with the apparent disregard of a child, having been washed, groomed and dressed immaculately, rolling in the flower bed outside the front door. Tell me about it, indeed.

. . . .

As soon as the transporters had returned to the factory the following day, the Williams-Renaults were taken apart. Closer examination of Hill's car revealed that a coupling on the left-rear drive shaft was showing more than the expected amount of wear. A press statement from the team announced the find and suggested that this could have contributed to Hill's undignified exit from the race. It was a characteristically direct move which spoke volumes for the team's integrity; others might easily have chosen to deal with the matter in private, leaving the driver to shoulder the opprobrium in public.

Certainly, it did much for Hill's peace of mind. If nothing else, it was a sound psychological move as Damon prepared to recover lost ground two weeks later in Hungary. He went to Budapest knowing that anything less than a win would be unacceptable. And he would have a brand new car to help him on his way.

In fact, the age and mileage of the car sitting in the left-hand side of the garage was of no concern to Hill as he slid into the cockpit for the first time on the Friday morning. The main thing was to ensure that it worked better than any of the other 23 machines being prepared for the opening practice session. And, as ever, David Brown, clipboard in hand, was there to help him do it.

Grand Prix racing portrays an image of thunderous noise and furious activity. You would have been surprised,

. . . .

therefore, by the relaxed start to the weekend. It was as if someone had forgotten to mention that the first free practice session actually began at 9.30 a.m. True, the times recorded would not count towards grid positions – that would have to wait until qualifying between 1 and 2 p.m. – but surely there was work to be done?

Indeed there was but the rules say that each driver is limited to just 23 laps in the 90-minute session, which is split at the halfway point by a 15-minute break. No point in rushing out, particularly at this circuit. The Hungaroring is hardly used (unlike, say, Silverstone, which is a scene of constant activity throughout the year) and the track is therefore dusty and dirty. Worse still, some demented mind had smashed glass onto the end of the pit straight. There was no point in being the first to check that the marshals had done a good job with their brooms and buckets.

David Coulthard did gentle stretching exercises at the back of the garage while Hill chatted with Brown and Patrick Head. The cars were ready, their engines silent, the mechanics fussing over minute details for the want of something better to do. It was hardly all rush and thunder. That would come in due course.

After several minutes of hanging about, Coulthard ventured onto the track, his first job being a radio check with his engineer, Jock Clear. The purpose was to establish that communication was viable all the way around the 2.46-mile circuit. Coulthard talked his way through the lap, the gentle Scottish burr occasionally developing a tremor as the harsh ride of the Williams reacted to the many bumps on the track surface.

'Into the bottom hairpin... second... third... fouuurrrrth... fifth...' the dialogue continuing all the way with perfect clarity, Ken Rumbold, the team's radio specialist, clearly having done his work. Hill followed suit not long after.

By 9.50 a.m., only four cars had completed flying laps, the rest, like Hill and Coulthard, having ventured back to the pit lane after a single lap. It seemed this session would never start, a feeling obviously shared by Patrick Head as he stood by the motor-home, parked on the lower level of the paddock and overlooking the return leg of the track. Jamming his thumb on the transmit button, the technical director spoke into his headset.

'David, what are your plans for going out?'

'Five minutes or so,' replied Brown. 'It's still very dusty at the last corner.'

Hill, sitting in the car, was just as anxious to get going before the break at 10.15 a.m. Employing typically old-fashioned phraseology associated more with cricket than motor racing, Hill said he wanted to use the clear track because there was bound to be a last-minute rush 'before tea'.

A nod from Brown, and the starter was connected to the rear of the car. The tranquil scene was totally shattered as the V10 burst into life once more, the concrete floor seeming to vibrate, the sound waves somehow managing to bounce around your rib cage. Serious action. At last.

A benefit of being a front-running team becomes apparent as soon as one of your cars ventures onto the track. The television cameras immediately lock on to it and the pictures, both from the trackside and the on-board cameras, are relayed back to the monitors in the garage. While Brown watches from the pit wall, the mechanics keep an eye on the television screens, the on-car shots of their man at work acting like a video game, even though the silent pictures of cockpit action do not even begin to come close to portraying the physical drama of the moment. That only becomes evident when the car, having done several laps, returns to the pits.

The driver's voice has risen an octave, his delivery and breathing that little bit faster than before. As for the car itself, a quick inspection by Brown as it is wheeled backwards into the garage reveals excessive wear near the outer edge of the left-rear tyre. Hill reports that the handling had been fine until the last lap, when the car suddenly developed oversteer.

The rough band of rubber (known as graining) on the rear tread tells the story. It's a worrying development at this early stage. Brown immediately gets on the radio and asks Dickie Stanford, who is standing at the pit wall, to check the tyres on Schumacher's car when it returns to the pits. Stanford reports an identical problem on the Benetton. That, at least, is some consolation and indicates that there is nothing radically wrong with the set-up on the Williams.

In fact, the problem will largely be solved as the weekend wears on and more rubber is laid on the track, thus reducing its abrasive nature. But, in the meantime, steps are taken during the 15-minute break to adjust the car's set-up in order to try to assist the tyres.

As the mechanics fit softer rear springs, Hill is leaning against the cabinet of tools at the back of the garage, his right elbow resting on top of a vice. Then he moves to the rear of the car and absently drums his fingers on the rear wing. The work could not be completed any faster. Hill knows that. But the sound of engines being fired up in the Benetton garage next door automatically increases the anxiety to get going again. There is always the thought that Schumacher is still 21 points ahead. We've just got to win . . . *got* to win.

Hill and Coulthard return to the track. Now Hill has understeer (the tendency for the car to plough straight on

∎∎∎∎∎∎∎∎∎∎∎∎∎∎∎∎∎∎∎∎∎∎∎∎∎∎∎∎∎∎∎∎∎∎∎∎∎

rather than turn into the corner) leading him to suggest that the front anti-roll bar may be too stiff. Wing settings are discussed, Patrick Head listening in to the debate, adding his views and then increasing the tempo a notch by announcing that Schumacher has just set the fastest lap so far. The times may be meaningless in terms of grid positions but they do indicate the latest state of play.

As the two Williams-Renaults sit side by side in the garage, the drivers' beady eyes, peering through the slots in their blue crash helmets, are fixed on the monitors which are constantly updating lap times. The place is now a hive of activity, 14 mechanics working briskly, two Renault engineers plugging their computers into the cars, technicians from the tyre and brake companies checking temperatures, recording the readings and passing the slips of paper to David Brown and Jock Clear. These are attached to their respective clipboards; more information to be examined and reviewed later in the day.

The engineers note every detail change that has been made. Each item is a clue when it comes to solving the puzzle of establishing the perfect car, or as near to perfect as they can get. Nothing is overlooked. A seemingly innocuous alteration or occurrence now can have a far-reaching effect later on. Every time the car turns a wheel, the engineers write about it, a series of techno-shorthand notes covering everything from the drivers' comments to

∎∎∎∎∎∎∎∎∎∎∎∎∎∎∎∎∎∎∎∎∎∎∎∎∎∎∎∎∎∎∎∎∎∎∎∎∎

the tyre pressures and temperatures, the wing angles, spring and damper settings. Even the weather. And, right now, the temperature is rising in every sense.

Gone is the casual air evident at the beginning of practice some 90 minutes earlier. Now the track is busy, the incessant noise unnoticed by Brown as his head-set muffles the racket and amplifies Hill's comments while lap times come down and further discoveries are made. The session ends with Schumacher fastest and Coulthard second. Hill is fourth, 0.7 seconds slower than the Benetton. There is some consolation from the fact that the Williams-Renaults have been among the quickest more or less from the outset. Schumacher, meanwhile, had spun twice in a desperate effort to refine the handling of the Benetton. But, of course, he is still 21 points ahead.

The number of laps during each qualifying session is limited to 12 per driver. Each lap, therefore, must be made to count, a restriction which is exacerbated by the fact that new tyres are only at their very best for one lap, maybe two.

There is a further complication this weekend: predictions suggest that tyre wear will be more critical than usual because of the abrasive track and possible high temperatures during the race. In other words, a driver may need more than the usual three or four sets to see him through on race day. But, of course, he only has seven sets for the entire weekend, so economy of use during practice and qualifying is paramount. And yet it is absolutely imperative that he sets the fastest qualifying time at this track because, with overtaking limited by the tight nature of the Hungaroring, grid positions are everything. A Grand Prix driver's job is not easy. 'Tell me about it,' smiles Damon.

Hill takes a gamble. In order to both save tyres and check the set-up of the car, he chooses to run a used set of tyres first time out during qualifying. It is his decision even though a fresh set would be faster. Brown can see Hill's point. But he can also appreciate the risk of running tyres which have passed their best at a time when the driver will be pushing harder than ever before.

'If you throw it in gravel at this stage, we're finished,' says Brown quietly, referring to the fact that once a car is stuck out on the circuit, there will be no means of retrieving it before the end of the session. And, because the use of spare cars is not allowed during practice, all it will need is for a wet final qualifying session on Saturday and Hill will be starting the race from the back of the grid.

Hill looks at his engineer as if to say, 'Yeah, David, I know that.' But as Brown points out afterwards, 'If I hadn't said it, and he spun off, I'd look a bit of a prat.' Quite.

As it is, they both look good. With the car sliding spectacularly, Hill not only brings it back in one piece, he

■ ■

establishes a time on used tyres which would ultimately have been worth seventh fastest had it been his only lap. It has been a measure of Hill's confidence both in himself and in the car. He says to Brown and Head, 'The balance of the car is good; we don't need to change anything.' An engineer doesn't hear that sort of statement very often but, when he does, it is music to his ears. And there are fresh tyres waiting.

Halfway through the 60-minute session, Schumacher sets the fastest time so far with a lap of 1 minute 19.490 seconds. Two minutes later and Hill leaves the pit lane. His first quick lap of 1 minute 18.446 seconds makes it clear that he has the measure of the Benetton. So, for that matter, has Coulthard as he goes round in 1 minute 19.000 seconds. 'Okay; P2,' says Jock Clear over the radio with the minimum of fuss or emotion as he refers to second-fastest time.

When Hill's car is pushed into the garage, Brown asks for another five kilograms of fuel to be added. Hill, meanwhile, is watching the television monitor as it carries pictures of Schumacher's ragged reply.

'There's something wrong with Schumacher's car,' says Hill.

'Can't drive, can he?' chortles Head.

'I've been telling you that all along,' says Hill. He's joking too. But only just.

■ ■

∎∎∎∎∎∎∎∎∎∎∎∎∎∎∎∎∎∎∎∎∎∎∎∎∎∎∎∎∎∎∎∎∎∎∎∎∎∎

Twelve minutes to go and Jean Alesi flies off the road, prompting the appearance of a red flag to bring the session to a temporary halt while the mess is cleared up. Everyone watches the replay of the accident, not from a morbid point of view but to see if anything can be learned. Hill suggests there might be oil on the track. Brown is on the radio to Dickie Stanford straight away.

'Can you ask Roland [Bruynseraede, the FIA's safety delegate] if there is oil before the corner? Looks like he lost it going in.' It turns out that Alesi did not need any assistance when it came to losing control of his Ferrari.

At the restart, Hill waits for as long as possible, the better to allow others to clean up the track. Watching the clock and doing a quick calculation, Brown works out that Hill will need to leave the pits in the next 40 seconds if he is to have time for two flying laps. Hill leaves with not a moment to spare. Schumacher can only manage a lap of 1 minute 19.490 seconds. Coulthard's 1 minute 19.000 seconds is worth second place but Hill gets down to 1 minute 18.374 seconds, putting provisional pole beyond doubt.

'Well done, Damon,' says Head. 'You did a very good job.'

'Thanks, Patrick. Let's see what happens tomorrow.'

He might have added, 'Let's see which way the wind blows.' Overnight, it turned through 180 degrees, blowing

∎∎∎∎∎∎∎∎∎∎∎∎∎∎∎∎∎∎∎∎∎∎∎∎∎∎∎∎∎∎∎∎∎∎∎∎∎∎

Schumacher sweeps past his adoring fans on his way to victory
at Hockenheim.

The old one-two. David Coulthard heads for second place in Hungary
to give Williams-Renault their first clean sweep of the season.

In an unaccustomed mid-field position, Schumacher rounds La Source to start the first lap of the mighty Spa-Francorchamps circuit.

David Coulthard found form but lost his oil in Belgium.

Some of the Williams factory team, clockwise, from top left:
Bob Torrie, Roger Tipler, Steve Berry and Jim Bennett, Judd Flogdell,
Terry Galt, Bernie Jones.

The sun shone on David Coulthard as he head

wards his first Grand Prix victory in Portugal.

Damon Hill, caught behind Alesi's Ferrari in Japan.

Talk, talk. Jock Clear (left) and David Brown discuss set-ups on the cars.
In the background Damon Hill compares notes with his Renault engineer,
Denis Chevrier.

Damon Hill tells Clive James about retaining pole position in Australia.
Ann Bradshaw eavesdrops with her tape recorder.

The travelling team. Robbie Campbell celebrates his last race with
pride of place in the team photograph in Adelaide.

For the seventeenth and last time. Hill (right) and Coulthard make good starts from the front row in Adelaide. Schumacher (behind Hill) is about to be engulfed by the red Ferraris.

Fond farewell. Hill dominates the final race on the streets of Adelaide.

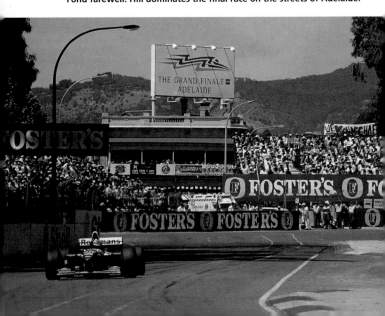

■ ■

down the straight instead of against the cars, the resulting push from behind running the engines against their limiters as they reach maximum revs more quickly than before; yet another variable for Brown and Clear to note and digest as free practice gets underway.

Now is the time to think about the set-up for the race and try running with more fuel on board in order to determine the effect of the extra weight on the handling and overall performance of the car.

Hill completes a run of seven laps before the 15-minute break. He climbs from the car, removes his helmet and flameproof balaclava, takes a swig from a bottle of water and worries about persistent understeer. His thick hair is pressed flat, the outer edge sticking to his face and neck as perspiration drips from his chin. Hill barely notices. That understeer is the cause of much discussion.

Meanwhile, Coulthard's engine has developed a misfire, prompting a bout of activity from the Champion representative, Simon Arkless, as he is called in to examine the spark plugs for any tell-tale evidence. It's technical stuff. 'Lots of shit on that one,' he says, removing his eye glass and pointing to one of the ten plugs arranged before him. The Renault engineers nod and return to their engine and their computers.

The misfire is cleared by the time the second half gets under way; Hill is happy with the adjustments which have

■ ■

• •

reduced the understeer. It's back to running a light load of fuel and thinking about final qualifying. Once again, Hill is quickest; Schumacher third, Coulthard fourth. The track is faster today, thanks to the laying down of more rubber. Hill has it all to do again if he is to maintain a pole position which is second only to Monaco in terms of strategical importance. Get into the lead, play your cards right, and no one will get by. That's the theory. In practice, it can be very different. Tell me about it.

Twenty minutes into qualifying and Coulthard is the first Williams driver to leave the pits.

'The track is a second quicker than yesterday,' says Clear. 'If your time is not up in that region, then abort the lap,' a reference to the split time which will appear on the dashboard readout and give Coulthard an indication of his progress.

There is no need to abandon the lap. Coulthard claims pole position for the time being with a lap of 1 minute 18.362 seconds. Schumacher has moved into second place with 1 minute 18.514 seconds.

Hill, waiting in the car, his mind focused completely on the task ahead, checks the monitor and then indicates to Brown that it is time to go. The start-up procedure begins once more.

Hill completes one lap (1 minute 18.579 seconds) before returning. He experienced a touch too much over-

• •

steer. There is a debate as to whether an attempt should be made to fix it in the time available.

'I certainly think you should go out again while the track is reasonably clear,' says Head. 'You are the only one of the top eleven who hasn't improved.'

A fresh set of tyres is fitted and fuel added. It is 1.35 p.m. There are 25 minutes left but, more important, there are only five cars on the track. Hill gives the signal to start his engine and off he goes.

1 minute 18.231 seconds.

'In, Damon,' says Brown. 'P1.'

Coulthard leaves as Hill returns. 'Didn't gain as much time as I expected to,' says Damon. 'A bit too much under-steer now.'

'Seventeen five eight eight; P1 for David,' booms Head.

Then, to add even more pressure, the monitors show Gerhard Berger in second place briefly, before being eclipsed by Schumacher with a 1 minute 18.085 second lap. Hill and Brown, meanwhile have discussed making changes to the rear springs. There is no time to lose since only 14 minutes remain.

'Have we done that?' asks Damon, jerking his thumb towards the rear of the car.

'We're doing it,' says Brown.

'Well,' replies Hill, stating the obvious for the want of

■ ■

something better to say, 'keep going.' Then a brief pause. 'Do I have time for two runs or not?'

'Yes. It's possible.' But Brown is now having to work out whether or not there will be time to refuel in between. The answer is yes. But it will be tight.

With ten minutes remaining, Hill leaves the pits. The order on the screen says Coulthard first, Schumacher second and Hill fifth.

Then Coulthard does a 1 minute 17.366 seconds. Schumacher improves to 1 minute 17.558 seconds. Hill is now on his first lap. His mechanics gather round the screen. The split times look good, the final figures even better: 1 minute 16.982 seconds! Brilliant!

Then Hill flies off the road at the first corner. But he regains the track and heads for the pits. Five minutes remain.

As the car is backed into the garage, Brown walks briskly towards the car, his thumb on the transmit button. 'What was that all about?' he asks crisply, literally in passing and not really expecting an answer. The tyres have to be changed and fuel added. The pace around the car is frantic, but controlled. Just about.

'You've got to get out in 1 minute 40 seconds,' says Head.

It's not over yet. As Hill rushes towards the pit lane exit, Schumacher is on another fast lap. The first split

■ ■

shows he is 0.107 seconds slower than Hill; the second says he is 0.528 seconds off Damon's time. But Schumacher does not give up. In fact he tries so hard that he spins coming on to the finishing straight. Hill's last lap is now academic. He has pole position.

Meanwhile poor Coulthard, convinced with good reason that he could have taken pole, failed to get out of the pit lane due to time lost over last-minute refuelling, an unfortunate and rare slip by the meticulous Clear. Coulthard's disappointment is compounded by Hill's obvious delight as the pole position Williams rolls to a halt in front of the garage.

Head is on the radio first.

'Good job, Damon,' he says. 'You gave us a few heart attacks along the way! But well done.' Hill explains that he had been anxious to see his lap time on the dashboard readout. When he looked up, he had sailed past his braking point for the first corner and was heading towards the gravel. But that will become a happy piece of history.

The talk – lots of it – from here on will be about tomorrow and the race. Having done their bit at the press conference, the drivers climb the transporter steps at 2.30 p.m. and join their engineers in the air-conditioned debriefing room. The door clicks shut. They will remain there for as long as it takes. By 6 p.m., Stanford can wait no longer and goes inside to retrieve the work list for each car. And still the talking continues, minds focused solely on the following day.

Brown and Clear leave their hotel in central Budapest at 7.15 on Sunday morning. By the time they reach the circuit 30 minutes later, the mechanics have already tucked into breakfast at the motor-home. There is time for the engineers to go through the paperwork resulting from the previous day's debrief, ensuring that everything is up to speed in every sense, in readiness for the 30-minute warm-up at 9.30 a.m.

But first, pit stop practice has been scheduled in the pit lane, with extra attention being focused on changing nose-cones, an indication of the bumping and barging likely to be induced by the numerous slow corners, par-ticularly on the first lap. The Benetton mechanics watch, good-natured laughter rippling from the pit next door as the Williams mechanics bump into each other during the nose-cone routine. Bob Davis, the Number 1 on Hill's car, and Carl Gaden, the chief mechanic, sort out their footwork, the next attempt going like clockwork. Brown, stopwatch in hand, observes dryly, 'Like Pan's People; it's lovely when it comes together!'

That done, Brown and Clear carry on with their race day routine. Brown outlines the schedule:

'I'll have a word with our tyre men and then check with Goodyear and go through the plan for the warm-up.

■ ■

Talk to Carl and make sure he knows what we want to do; talk to the mechanics to make sure the car is in the condition you expect it to be in for the warm-up. We usually run the spare car for the first time, as well as the race car, during the warm-up and that's certainly the case here in Hungary.

'Then you find the driver – who normally arrives a bit later than we do – and go through the plan for the warm-up, discussing what we are going to use in the way of tyres, how much fuel we plan to run, are there any tests we want to carry out, or are we just going to run the car and play it by ear as it comes. Normally, there will be a check of some kind; it could be trying a different amount of wing, or revised engine mapping; something like that.

'After the warm-up, the engineers will sit down with both drivers and hold a debrief. First of all, are there any problems with the car which need fixing, because you have only got a limited amount of time. The first thing you need to establish is that there's nothing mechanically wrong with the car. Then we move on to the performance of the car and we decide whether we are going to make further changes for the race. If that is the case, then we will probably want to complete a number of laps before finally going to the grid. And, if so, how many. And are we then going to make more changes in the pit lane or will they be made on the grid, after which there is no

■ ■

further chance of trying out these changes before the start of the race.

'Following the debrief, we split up. The drivers either go and carry out PR work with the sponsors, or eat their pasta and go to sleep. The engineers return to the garage and go over the cars again.'

The drivers and engineers may have gone their separate ways, but the race is the only thing occupying their thoughts. Brown is soon in another meeting.

'About two hours before the start of the race,' he says, 'we will have a meeting with Renault, which is a similar sort of thing to the driver debrief. We go through a list of items, mainly to establish that we all agree on our race strategy; the plan for the number of laps before going to the grid; how much fuel we are going to run at the beginning of the race; do we have any mechanical problems; what's the oil consumption like; and so on.

'We will have already discussed tactics with the drivers but, if it is a bit of a close call between, say, one stop or two, we might go back to the driver and ask: "Okay, have you thought about this in more detail?" or "Have you considered that?" All the while, we will have been gathering more information and we can say to the driver: "Look, we think that other people are going to stop twice, therefore maybe we should adopt such-and-such a plan." We would come to some sort of conclusion, even if it is flexible and subject to last-minute change, depending on the latest information we have available.

'Whatever the decision, by this stage the mechanics will know when we intend to stop for tyres and how much fuel should be put in the cars and into the refuelling rigs. The tyre people will know which sets we plan to run.

'Once the pit lane opens, thirty minutes before the start of the race, we have fifteen minutes before it closes in which to fit in as many laps (via the pit lane, because people are already standing on the starting grid) we feel we need. After the pit lane closes, if we are still in the pits, then hard luck. It's too late to go to the grid. So, keeping a careful eye on the time, each driver might have done three or four laps, depending on whether there were changes to be checked or tyres which needed to be scrubbed in.

'Overall, the engineers check that the car is working okay; that the driver is happy. Talk to Renault once more about fuel; discuss tyre pressures with the tyre man; wander around on the grid to see what other people are doing with their wing settings; talk to the driver again about what he is going to do in the race and any other last-minute points that come up, such as possible changes to the weather.'

In Hungary, there was no need for that. The conditions

▪▪▪▪▪▪▪▪▪▪▪▪▪▪▪▪▪▪▪▪▪▪▪▪▪▪▪▪▪▪▪▪▪▪▪

remained blisteringly hot and conversation was about one thing; how many times would Schumacher stop?

Hill, Head and Brown had toyed with every option. Assuming Damon made a decent start, he could run with a heavy load of fuel and, since overtaking would be next to impossible, he would dictate the pace and nullify any ideas Schumacher might have about running light in the opening stages. On the other had, extra weight would make the tyres work harder. It would also make the car less nimble when overtaking back markers. The bottom line was that Damon had to win this race if he was to do anything about Schumacher's lead in the championship. It was not the time to take strategic risks. Three stops it would be.

But what of Schumacher? Would Benetton consider only making two stops? Unlikely, since Schumacher would want to attack. But nobody at Williams could be certain of that. Much would depend on the start.

Hill's cause was helped straightaway when both Williams drivers made perfect starts and denied Schumacher the chance to snatch the lead on the run to the first corner. Hill set to work immediately, extending his advantage to eight seconds in as many laps. He had to press on in case Schumacher, presently stuck behind Coulthard, was planning to stop just twice.

There was little for David Brown to communicate verb-

▪▪▪▪▪▪▪▪▪▪▪▪▪▪▪▪▪▪▪▪▪▪▪▪▪▪▪▪▪▪▪▪▪▪▪

ally to Hill during these early stages, which was not a problem because it was preferable to rely on the information displayed on the boards hung over the pit wall rather than risk breaking the driver's concentration.

Brown, stationed at the wall, would note the information appearing on the TAG-Heuer monitor and record Hill's lap times and the gaps to Coulthard and Schumacher on his race sheet. Stuart Mulley, the mechanic who handles Hill's board, would glance at the race sheet and transfer the information to the signalling board.

'Normally,' says Brown, 'only the race engineers will speak to the drivers. But I would not talk to the driver unless there is something which I think he ought to know. 'sually, it is as a back-up to the information on the pit board. But, in Hungary, we talked a lot because there was quite a bit to say, particularly after lap thirteen.'

That was when Schumacher overtook Coulthard and moved into second place. Hill had to know immediately the sort of lap times Schumacher was capable of now that he was unimpeded. This would be the first clue to how many stops the Benetton would be making.

The answer straightaway seemed to be three, judging by Schumacher's speed as he began to close down the 15-second gap to Hill. Confirmation came when Hill and Schumacher both stopped at the end of lap 17. They rejoined, Hill's lead reduced to eight seconds. At the end of lap 26, Brown was on the radio with the news that Schumacher had stopped early for a second time. This was not following the usual script.

The Williams team's curiosity had been aroused when Schumacher's first stop had been more than two seconds faster than Hill's. Then, just afterwards, someone spotted fuel leaking from the Benetton rig; it seemed that not all of the fuel had reached the car. Suspicions were strengthened when the Benetton team then prepared Johnny Herbert's refuelling rig (one which was known to be slower than the rig used by Schumacher) for their Number 1 driver's unscheduled early second arrival. It was clear now that he had to come in because there was very little fuel left in the car's tank due to the short measure at the first stop.

Brown did his best to relay all this to Hill without either confusing or alarming his driver. Above all, though, Brown kept Hill accurately informed about the size of his lead and the progress of his rival.

As the 77-lap race reached the halfway mark, Hill did not need to be told about Schumacher's whereabouts since the Benetton was darting around in his mirrors. Having made his second of three stops on schedule, Hill found that the sequence of events had allowed Schumacher to catch up. This was a critical phase. Each driver had one stop remaining but, because Schumacher had stopped early, he was running with less fuel at this point. Hill had to keep him back at all costs.

Not only did Hill succeed, he managed to open a commanding lead once the third and final stops had been and gone. The verbal communication between engineer and driver wound down to the point where Brown could rely once more on the pit board to give Hill the information he needed. And the board said '+10.3 Schu – L12' indicating he was leading Schumacher by 10.3 seconds with 12 laps to go.

Eight laps later and no Schumacher, Hill's day being made complete as he passed the stricken Benetton, parked on the grass with a broken fuel pump. Not only was Damon about to win, the championship gap had now been cut from 21 to 11 points. In theory, anyway. Hill would not allow himself to think about any of that until he had completed the final lap. Then the emotion swept over him. This may have been the twelfth victory of his career but it was also one of the most important – particularly after events in the previous two races. He was ecstatic.

A sea of arms greeted Hill from the Williams pit, Patrick Head booming his congratulations across the radio waves, the technical director's pleasure being rounded off by second place for Coulthard, the first one-two finish for the team in almost a year.

Hill dealt with the television interviews and the press conferences before retreating immediately to the motor-home. The intensity of concentration and effort required during an hour and three-quarters' work on a circuit without a straight worthy of the name had taken its toll. Particularly in this heat. Hill stretched out on the leather settee, the only sound being the soothing hum of the air-conditioning.

When David Brown arrived, Hill was being revived by a massage and a cup of tea. Both men were grinning. Not a lot needed to be said.

After a pause, Brown spoke: 'What about the car, Damon – any comments?'

The work must go on. Tell me about it.

CHAPTER SIX

LIKE TALKING
TO MUM

BELGIUM AND ITALY

Steve Fraser was 25 on the weekend of the Italian Grand Prix and he and his wife had been invited to join a birthday celebration in Cumbria. They had been looking forward to a few days off. But such straightforward pleasures do not take into account the uncompromising demands of motor racing.

On Friday, 8 September, Steve Fraser was as far removed from the solitude of the Lakes as it was possible to be. Monza on Grand Prix weekend is not, by any stretch of the imagination, a holiday for those who have to work in the midst of such ardent chaos. It is a rowdy theatre of sport where high paddock fences and hyperactive security guards fail to keep out the feeling that this is a sports venue of passion and tradition. It is a great place to be if you love Formula One.

That was no consolation to Mrs Fraser. Her husband's job as an electronics technician meant he was needed in Monza after dashboard modifications had developed a fault during a test at Imola a few days previously. Steve had not been to a race before. It was unfortunate that the request should come on this weekend in particular; it is a difficult one to explain to a wife of three months. 'She's a bit pissed off,' was the closest Fraser would come to hinting at the stress motor racing puts on any relationship, new or long established.

Such conflicts of interest are not confined to the race team, on the move for at least a third of the year. Factory personnel may be home-based but they, too, are subjected to intense surges of productivity, most notably when the new cars are being built at the beginning of the season, and when major modifications are introduced at a later stage. On such occasions, the work force is expected to produce the goods, no matter how many hours it may take. The period around the Belgian and Italian Grands Prix was a case in point.

Patrick Head and Adrian Newey had instigated a programme of substantial changes to the gearbox and rear suspension of FW17 and the developments had begun to reach hard metal in July and August. Tests at Silverstone had proved the alterations to be worthwhile in terms of decreased lap times. Now the modifications had to be put into production and fed into the already busy race programme.

Bob Torrie's office is the hub of production operations. Tall and soft-spoken, Bob is in charge of all sub-assembly; items such as the transmission, the wheel uprights and brakes. But, more than that, he is responsible for logistics; the art of making sure that everything is in the right place at the right time. Torrie must keep an eye on the test programme and ensure that developments resulting from it are put into production. The correct parts, produced to the precise specification, must be available when needed, and all this must mesh in with the routine work of race preparation and the schedule of replacement parts.

Bob is assisted by the paperwork produced by David Brown and Jock Clear as they log the mileage recorded during a race weekend and list the faults which will call for new or revised parts. A 'Build Sheet' for each car will detail the precise requirements for the next race and, at the time of Spa and Monza, all this was going on while, in the background, test sessions were taking place involving the new gearbox and suspension.

The gearbox alone placed a huge burden on the manufacturing side and two of them were required for the test at Imola a few days prior to the Italian Grand Prix. At least Torrie had the comforting back-up of standards and systems which he had evolved during years spent on the workshop floor of Williams Grand Prix Engineering. Eighteen years, to be precise.

Bob Torrie had been one of the first to join Frank and Patrick when they established the team in a small industrial unit in Station Road, Didcot. Torrie had worked as a mechanic at Lotus and he knew of Frank Williams and his indefatigable enthusiasm. 'Frank had very little money,' recalls Bob, 'but you knew that if he had 10p in his pocket, he would spend it on his motor racing. His enthusiasm was, and still is, incredibly infectious. My first job at Station Road was to paint the dark green walls white and my first technical question to Patrick Head was "One coat, or two?" '

At the time, WGPE consisted of no more than five people but as the scope and ambition of the team grew, so did the need to have a properly supervised sub-assembly area. Bob, having undergone a back operation, was no longer fit enough to travel and he was chosen for the job. 'Apart from doing a few test sessions, I was home-based,' he recalls. 'And I hated it. But you soon learn to adjust.'

Today, the team could not afford to let Bob out of its sight for long. Instead of asking the questions, he answers them. The walls of his office, located to one side of the workshop, are lined with more than 400 boxes of transmission parts. He knows them all intimately. A technician will arrive, brandishing a drawing and holding a part that is not suitable for the job. One look from Torrie and the problem is solved. 'No, what you've got there is an eleven-fifty-three. You'll need a seven and eight for that,' he says, automatically reaching for a box the contents of which are subtly different to the one next to it.

Designing and building racing cars is all about specialization. It is the art of mix and match, but with a precision which would bring out the average engineering company in a cold sweat. A good fit is not enough. It must be perfect, as must the skills of the technicians themselves. And the workshop at Williams is brim-full of them.

Roger Tipler is a foreman who leads by example. His skills with sheet metal are second to none and, in late August, there was no better example of his expertise than his intricate work on the radiators for the new gearbox.

Radiator cores are designed by Williams and manufactured by specialists but it is one of Tipler's jobs to produce the aluminium tanks at each end and construct the radiators themselves. Apart from having to fit within the tight confines of bodywork and chassis, the intricately shaped tanks have to withstand huge temperature variations as well as internal pressures of between thirty and forty pounds per square inch. The flow of liquid, be it water or oil, must have no turbulence and yet the tanks must tuck neatly around both ends of the core. Each tank is made from two pieces, the immaculate welding by Tipler being typical of his manufacturing creed of keeping 'everything tidy and right'.

Tipler, 15 years with Williams, had worked for Pressed Steel before branching into motor racing by joining JW Automotive in the days when the Slough-based team dominated world sportscar racing. Roger answered Williams's advertisement for a welder/fabricator when that particular trade was at full stretch in any racing enterprise. The demise of the aluminium chassis in favour of carbon composites has since diminished the sheet-metal worker's scope, but the work that remains – suspension, radiators, exhausts – is as intricate and as vital as before.

When Tipler joined Williams, there was no supervisory control on the factory floor and his role as foreman more or less evolved as the company grew, Roger handling everything bar chassis manufacture, which was under the supervision of Bernie Jones, one of the team's longest serving employees.

In keeping with many on the shop floor, Jones served his apprenticeship in the aircraft industry before answering an advertisement in a local newspaper in 1977. Bernie's first love was, and still is, motorcycles, but the

challenge of making the aluminium chassis for a fledge-
ling Grand Prix team was intriguing.

'In my first year, there were four chaps and me,' says
Jones. 'It was a case of designing our own jig and getting
on with it. Even now, with the composite chassis, the
whole chassis is set up on a jig and I continue to design
them. But, as in most things with motor racing, there is
plenty of variety. You never know what you will be doing
next. All you know is that, whatever it is you are asked
to do, you use your initiative and just get on with it. The
great thing is that you get to see the finished article; you
see the car go racing and you know your efforts are worth
something. But it doesn't half piss you off when you see
the car break down . . .'

Jones had suffered that agony while watching the
Belgian Grand Prix on television a few days earlier. In fact,
frustration had been evident everywhere within Williams
at the end of another controversial and dramatic weekend,
and much of it had to do with the typically fickle weather
at Spa-Francorchamps.

Damon Hill had been keen to continue the momentum
of a brilliant win in Hungary and yet his progress throughout the two days of practice at Spa had been characterized
by indecision and minor driving errors. They had come
at an inopportune time, particularly a spin at the end of
final qualifying, just as the track was drying out after a

short, sharp shower of rain. Had he not gone off, Hill would have been able to capitalize on a disastrous weekend so far for Schumacher, the championship leader having crashed his car in the morning practice session.

David Coulthard, on the other hand, had suddenly found form when he needed it most. His promising reputation had been open to question following fairly average performances in Germany and Hungary but, at Spa, he settled into the groove and claimed fifth on the grid. Hill was eighth – his lowest position in three years – but Schumacher was even worse off in sixteenth place.

The promise of an intriguing race was duly fulfilled – but with the seemingly inevitable smear of controversy at the end of it. Hill and Schumacher eventually found their way to the head of the field but the advent of rain threw the race wide open once more. Hill chose to stop for wet tyres while Schumacher gambled on the track drying out and such were the changing circumstances that both decisions seemed correct at various points within a five-minute period.

The problem for Hill was that Schumacher would not let the Williams through even though Damon, on grooved rain tyres on a still wet track, was plainly the quicker of the two. By the time Hill found a way past, the track was drying and the pendulum was swinging just as rapidly in Schumacher's direction. Then, just for good measure, Hill would earn a ten-second stop-go penalty for speeding in the pit lane when he came to change from wet tyres to slicks.

A recovery to second place was of no interest to Damon after the race as he climbed from his car and told Schumacher what he thought about the Benetton driver's questionable tactics during that crucial stage. The stewards later agreed with Hill and gave Schumacher a one-race ban, suspended for four races. It amounted to no more than a slap on the wrist and, by then, the damage had been done; Schumacher was 15 points ahead in the championship.

If the rights and wrongs of the incident were of no more than academic interest to Bernie Jones, he had been mortified to watch the Williams of Coulthard grind to a smoky halt while leading the race. This was far more serious; a blow to the collective midriff of the workshop floor at Didcot. The unspoken question in every mind was: 'What broke – and was it my bit?'

What made the failure seem even worse was the fact that Coulthard had been driving beautifully. The Scotsman looked to have the race under easy control. He was six seconds ahead and going away when the gearbox lost all of its oil after 16 laps. But at least the workforce could rest easy, the failure in the oil feed pipe having been caused by Coulthard's car receiving a bump in the rear during the scuffle through the very tight La Source hairpin seconds after the start. Even so, this was not the result the team had been looking for.

With Spa-Francorchamps being the closest continental circuit to Didcot, the three Williams transporter trucks were backed up to the side entrance of the workshops first thing on the Monday morning after the race. The unloading went almost unnoticed as the factory staff continued their efforts to produce the latest modifications, while making preparations in time to have the trucks leave the following weekend for the 1,500-mile run to Italy. Use of the word 'industrious' would not make a start on it. Indeed, it was easy to see why Williams Grand Prix Engineering had twice won the Queen's Award for Industry.

For the first award ceremony in 1981, Frank Williams showed typical feeling and understanding for his 'boys' by arranging to have Bob Torrie and Bernie Jones represent the workforce at Buckingham Palace. Bernie still hasn't quite got over it.

'Wonderful,' he says, wistfully. 'We met the Queen. She was brilliant. She'd really done her homework; knew all about the team. She was so nice. It was just like talking to your mum . . .'

Bernie spoke with such enthusiasm that it seemed feasible to suppose that Her Majesty would know that the exhaust system on one side of the Renault V10 comprised 40 sections, from the cylinder head to the tip of the tail pipe.

Certainly, each and every one of those pieces was engraved in the subconsciouses of Steve Berry and Jim Bennett, since they had been responsible for the design and manufacture of these convoluted snake-pits of metal. Seeing how they had crammed five pipes – each the same length – into the limited space was a testimony to unique skills which had been largely self-taught. Berry had come from British Leyland, where he worked on door skins and bonnets, to work as a fabricator for Williams; Bennett, an apprentice with an aircraft company, had heard about Williams because his brother used to work for Frank. Jim and Steve found themselves more or less drifting into the exhaust pipe section: 'I was asked if I would like to do exhausts,' says Steve, 'and I thought, "Why not?" That was it, really.'

Berry and Bennett have been working as a team for more than six years, and during that period they have elevated their trade to an art form. The pipes themselves are made from Inconel, a nickel zinc alloy which is more stable than stainless steel (the material formerly used to manufacture exhausts) when temperatures reach 850°C. But the downside is the fact that Inconel is very difficult to work with. 'It's tough,' says Bennett. 'Hit it with a hammer and it springs back.'

Having designed the layout (using cardboard hoses) to make sure it fits between the floor pan and the underside of the engine, and having received the approval of Renault, Berry and Bennett set about making it. It can take two days just to produce the collector (the point where five exhausts merge into one), a jewel of craftsmanship requiring welding on both the outside and within the very cramped interior of the collector. A minimum of six complete exhaust sets is required for each race weekend. That's a lot of bending and welding. And doubtless the odd spot of cursing, given the stubborn intransigence of Inconel.

Further along the workshop floor, in among the towering milling machines, Terry Galt exercises similar delicate skills even if, at first sight after visiting Tipler, Bennett and Berry, this would appear to be the stone mason's controlled violence compared to the nimble fingers of a jeweller. Despite the advance of computerized precision in Galt's trade, manual milling, boring and tapping are still required when it comes to manufacturing the suspension components and many of the intricate bits and pieces unique to a Grand Prix car. Racing machinery requires close tolerances, a fact which Terry Galt understood from the outset since he had always been a motor racing fan when working at Harwell, and then as a contract engineer, before joining Williams in 1991.

'It's a brilliant company to work for,' says Galt. 'I wish I had come here sooner. I always follow the races on television and, of course, it means even more to me now that I am with Williams. You see one of our cars going round and round and you can say to yourself: "I've done a lot of the parts on that." It's a nice feeling. But it's heartbreaking when you see them get crunched.' Terry would be cringing in his seat when the television pictures came through from the Gran Premio d'Italia.

The weekend at Monza had started on an encouraging note. Coulthard had taken provisional pole on Friday, with Hill third fastest and feeling much happier with his car. In fact, there was not a lot wrong with FW17, so much so that Dickie Stanford was spared the sometimes desperate phone calls to Didcot.

Part of the team manager's role is to maintain constant contact with headquarters, updating and advising of latest developments and disasters, speaking to key people such as Alan Challis, the production/race team coordinator. As a former mechanic with BRM in the 1960s and then crew chief with Williams, Challis is one of the most experienced men in the place.

'I keep in contact with Alan all the time,' says Stanford. 'I'll say something like: "We've tried this part, or we've run that, it's been okay and now we need some more made as soon as possible." Alan will put that in hand and then Donna [Robertson] will arrange shipment to wherever we are. I'll also be talking to Tony Pilcher, the production manager, and to people such as Steve Wise, because he deals with electronics, and John Sutton, who designs the gearboxes. I'll also be passing on the latest developments to Brian Lambert, who leads the test team. But so far this weekend, it's been pretty quiet. A fatal thing to say, I suppose . . .'

Indeed, the night before, Friday, had been routine, the mechanics rolling down the garage shutters at the very respectable hour of 8.30 p.m. This was worrying. Life in the pit lane is never that smooth and Stanford's prophecy was about to come true as the cars blasted round the autodrome during free practice on Saturday morning.

A bolt fell into the air intake on Hill's Renault V10. Unfortunately, as it dropped into one of the cylinders, it met the piston on the way up. The resulting explosion was as savage as the firing pin of a gun hitting the business end of a bullet. The cylinder block managed to contain a major part of the hugely destructive forces but even so, the damage was considerable, oil, water and fragments of metal appearing in places where they had no right to be.

The errant bolt was a Renault problem rather than a

slip-up by Williams but the engine manufacturer had no reason to feel ashamed; this was the first engine failure they had experienced in almost two years, an astonishing record considering the stresses and strains involved, and a testament to the extent of their superior performances. There was absolutely no acrimony on either side, mainly because there was no time for it. Hill's engine had to be changed very quickly if he wanted to improve on his grid position during final qualifying.

The team threw themselves into action, everyone, including mechanics who could be spared from Coulthard's car, doing whatever they could. Under normal, less frantic circumstances, the job would be completed in two hours. The Williams lads had the fresh V10 installed in an hour and twenty minutes. Hill was able to take part in a qualifying session which saw Coulthard put pole position beyond doubt with a succession of brilliant laps, Damon having to make do with fourth on the grid after running wide while pushing hard in a bid to catch up.

Steve Fraser, the electronics technician diverted from the Lake District to Monza, had helped with the mopping up of oil and water which had found its way to the garage floor. Similarly David Williams, an unfamiliar figure at the race track, had rolled up his sleeves, glad of the opportunity to assist by topping up brake fluid and generally attempting to keep the place tidy in the midst of such controlled chaos.

Williams is general manager of the company. As such, he is responsible for all manufacturing, organization, research and development, facilities, personnel and any commercial projects outside the running of the team. A former general manager at Hunting Aerospace, Williams was hired in 1988 when Patrick Head decided the company needed a professional to run the factory as its technology base and facilities expanded. Williams sees his job as providing the infrastructure, thus allowing Head and Frank Williams to worry about making the cars go faster.

David Williams also looks ahead several years and tries to ensure that the team will have the necessary technology to deal with whatever may be required in the future. Of more immediate concern during the summer of 1995 was the plan to quit the premises in Basil Hill Road and move to a new factory on a 32-acre site seven miles away in the village of Grove. This would not be a case of backing a couple of vans to the front door, supplying tea and biscuits to a gang of hairy-chested removal men and then simply turning up at Grove the next day and expecting to carry on as before. It would be a military manoeuvre on the grand scale. David Williams would have to ensure as little disruption as possible while the team worked on FW18 and prepared for the 1996 season. It was a tall order

• •

but Williams was fortunate in being able to call upon the assistance of one of the team's sponsors, Andersen Consulting, a £2bn management and technology consulting organization capable of advising on the most practical way of moving 224 full-time staff and their equipment.

'The entire process is complex,' said Williams, 'but two parts of the move are particularly important. We've got to ensure that the Computer-Aided Design system is available up to the very moment it leaves, and operational at the new site immediately. It is our prime design tool and our engineering programmes are entirely dependent on it.

'The second is moving the composite plant and autoclaves which bake our fibre parts. Williams has a unique capability in this area; it is so particular to us that we cannot sub-contract it. The help we're getting from Andersen Consulting is extremely valuable to us. They introduced skills we don't have, and didn't even realize we needed.'

The beauty of dealing with a racing team is that the employees are mentally attuned to taking the unusual in their stride. This is not a nine-to-five job and the company will go to great lengths to ensure prospective team members fully appreciate that.

'We try to give each new recruit to the factory a week's trial,' says David Williams. 'We ask them to come in after work or in the evenings, just to see what they can do.

• •

■■

Everyone, regardless of their ability, then goes through a Starter Grade before moving on to Grade One and, during that time, we will see how they react to the pressures which occur at various times of the year.

'More than anything, you need to have your family behind you,' Williams goes on. 'People need to understand what is involved with a racing team. And, of course, the interest has got to be there, otherwise you will find this is a helluva hard job for the money!'

That dedication was unexpectedly questioned and then reinforced under desperately tragic circumstances in May 1994. The death of Ayrton Senna may have stunned the world of motor racing but it tore into the very fabric of Williams Grand Prix Engineering. This was the first time a driver had lost his life at the wheel of a Williams product. It brought the desperate realization that motor racing really can be a highly dangerous business and, once the initial shock had subsided, deeply difficult questions were asked in moments of personal reflection.

What made it even harder to bear – or on the other hand, it may have helped in some instances – was the fact that Ayrton had spent an entire day at the factory, a visit designed to not only bring him into personal contact with the people behind the scenes in his new team, but also to boost morale after a very difficult start during the first two races of the season. Senna had impressed everyone

■■

with his understanding, his civility, his firm belief that, together, they could get the job done. He had posed for official photographs with staff at every point along the way. The pictures arrived a week after the accident at Imola.

'We still haven't got over the shock,' says David Williams. 'I can't tell you how much Ayrton impressed everyone that day and, of course, that made the whole thing even harder to take. On the other hand, we feel we know him so much better than before. But that does not answer the question of how to cope with such devastating circumstances. Most people just hurled themselves into their job and attempted to work their way through it. There are no easy answers.'

Judd Flogdell came face-to-face with reality sooner than most of the factory-based staff. Responsible for the electronic hardware on the cars, Judd had to spend the Monday after Imola delving into the data the team had received from Ayrton's car in the hope of finding a clue to the cause of the accident. 'It was pretty awful,' she says, recalling a task which brought an entirely different perspective to the business of working with data analysis units. Certainly, it was not a task she had envisaged when entering motor racing with Williams in March 1992.

Judd was working in the audio business while sharing a house with two mechanics from Benetton. The chance of joining Williams offered the opportunity of doing something completely new and her expertise brought a job with Steve Wise in the electronics division, her brief covering dashboard displays, gearbox control units and sensors such as accelerometers and load cells.

During the course of her induction, Judd had been made aware of the risk element in the sport; it could hardly be avoided thanks to the constant reference to safety standards which are critical in terms of drivers' lives. Even so, the events of 1 May 1994 were to leave a lasting impression.

'It was a big shock,' says Judd. 'The death of Roland Ratzenberger on the Saturday had been upsetting and I tried to comprehend how members of his team would feel – but I couldn't. Then I found out for myself the next day. It actually seemed to get worse as the week went on. There were loads of letters and faxes; many of them were very touching.'

Flowers continue to arrive regularly at the factory, a reminder both of the man and of the hazards of the business he had dominated with such exquisite artistry. Ayrton Senna would have been the first to realize and accept that, even in the face of such mind-numbing tragedy, life must go on. The calendar will not go into reverse. If anything, it accelerates by dragging you into the desperate reality of a sport which suddenly seems to have become a cold and calculating business. But the neat Senna 'S' insignia on the nose of each Williams gives a subtle reminder of respect for the past as the team continues its headlong pursuit of success in the future.

The chances of that happening at Monza took a surprising turn for the worse when David Coulthard spun – while on his way to the starting grid. As the pole position man covered himself in embarrassment the race started without him, but then luck swung Coulthard's way just as dramatically, when a first-lap accident caused the race to be stopped and allowed David to take the fresh start in the spare car.

Undaunted by the fact that this car had been set up for his team-mate, Coulthard resisted heavy pressure from Berger's Ferrari and, once he had settled down and got used to the car, David began to ease away, leaving Berger to fend off Schumacher in the Benetton.

Coulthard began to set a string of fastest laps but the chances of that first win for the Scotsman suddenly disappeared when a broken wheel bearing – a most unexpected failure – sent him off the road and, ultimately, into retirement after just 14 laps.

Hill, meanwhile, had closed on Schumacher as they disputed what had now become second place behind Berger's leading Ferrari. Hill seemed able to close on the Benetton at will. On lap 24, he got a bit too close.

■■■■■■■■■■■■■■■■■■■■■■■■■■■■■■■■■■■■

The championship contenders came across the Arrows of Taki Inoue as they rushed through the 170 m.p.h. Curva Grande. Schumacher went round the outside of the Arrows, passing Inoue on the left before cutting back across. As Hill tried to do likewise, Inoue moved left, forcing Hill to move right and begin to draw alongside. As he did so, Hill realized that Inoue was not aware of his presence.

By now, they were into the braking area for the second-gear chicane at Curva della Roggia. Hill momentarily eased off the brakes to allow the Williams to surge forward and make Inoue realize that an accident was inevitable if the Japanese driver continued to veer towards his right. Inoue got the message but, as Hill braked hard once more, he was suddenly aware of the rapidly advancing rear end of a Benetton.

In trying to avoid one accident, Hill had got himself involved in another. Unfortunately, it was Schumacher he was ramming off the road. Under normal circumstances, this would have been judged a 'racing accident'. But these were not normal circumstances; certainly, not in the eyes of the media. This was War.

For the Williams team members present at the circuit, and the workforce watching television at home, it was not quite as serious as that. But it was a disaster none the less; a poor return on more than 23,000 man hours since the

■■■■■■■■■■■■■■■■■■■■■■■■■■■■■■■■■■■■

• •

previous race in Belgium. At least at Spa they had come away with some points. The only battle Williams won at Monza was the race to be first to get away from that boisterous place on the Sunday night. Steve Fraser's dashboard ministrations had been successful, but he might as well have enjoyed a few days off in the Lake District.

• •

■ ■

CHAPTER SEVEN

BRINGING HOME
THE BACON

PORTUGAL AND EUROPE

David Coulthard was talking about the Williams team.
'Yes,' he said quietly, 'I'm very disappointed to be leaving.
I've been with the team for quite a while; nearly three
years, including the time I've been test driver. I've got to
know everyone at the factory – almost by first name. I've
had a fantastic opportunity with Williams; starting your
career with a team like this doesn't happen very often.
That's why I want to make the most of it. I'll be very
disappointed if I don't win in a Williams; it's a very good
car. This race in Portugal is the thirteenth round of the
championship and, looking back, I really wish now that I
had won in Argentina last March.'

A lot had happened – or not, in Coulthard's case –
since he had claimed pole and led that race in Buenos

■ ■

Aires before mechanical trouble had intervened. A bout of tonsillitis, followed by an operation in June, had taken its toll. Coulthard had been frequently out-qualified by his team-mate, a lacklustre race performance in Germany marking a new low.

'I had such a bad period when I was sick mid-season,' admitted Coulthard. 'From Argentina onwards, my training programme was virtually non-existent. It is impossible to compete at this level when you are unfit. Now I am getting back into it: I am stronger and fitter and my mind is sharper.'

First signs of the come-back had been in Monza where he took pole position for the second time and, apart from the faux-pas when he spun off during the parade lap, drove confidently and quickly until, once again, mechanical problems brought his race to a premature end. Then came a welcome change to his routine.

Williams had chosen not to take up the option on Coulthard's contract (or, put another way, the McLaren team was perhaps exercising its right to have the Scotsman following a legal tussle between the two teams at the end of 1994) and Jacques Villeneuve, the 1995 Indycar Champion and winner of the Indianapolis 500, had been signed by Williams to take Coulthard's place in 1996. With the Indycar season now at an end, Frank Williams was keen to give the French-Canadian driver as much experience as possible; as a result, Coulthard's testing duties were not as onerous during the period following the Italian Grand Prix.

David put the time to good use in Monaco by extending the work on his fitness. Certainly, driving a Formula One car is training in itself, but mainly from a muscular point of view. Cardiographic work for endurance requires effort in the gym and Coulthard duly sweated it out. He arrived in Portugal feeling better, both mentally and physically, than he had all year thanks to peak fitness, and the fact that he had been quick at Monza. With only five races remaining on the calendar, he wanted more than ever to take pole position and score that elusive first victory.

Drivers usually like to arrive on the day before practice begins in order to take the opportunity to talk to team members in relative peace and tranquillity about latest developments and plans for the weekend, then perhaps have a word with the press and generally catch up on the latest gossip. Strangely, given his determination to do well, Coulthard was not seen all day Thursday at the Estoril circuit.

David's flight from Nice had arrived late and when he left Lisbon airport in his Renault hire car, he drove straight into a traffic jam. Since his girlfriend, Andrea Murray, accompanied by her mother and her sister, was on a later flight which was due in an hour's time, Coulthard returned to the airport to wait for them.

'Normally, I wouldn't have done that,' explained David. 'But the traffic was so bad, it made sense to return to the airport. I phoned the circuit, spoke to Frank, checked that everything was okay, and had a word with Jock. We'd had a long discussion earlier in the week about what we were going to do with the set-up on the car. I was happy that everything was okay and there was nothing I had missed; there was no reason for me to battle my way to the track, so we went straight to the hotel. I actually felt very relaxed.

'Usually,' he went on, 'you plan to go to the track for an hour, but by the time you stop to speak to everyone you bump in to, you are there for four or five hours. In any case, there was a team dinner that night to celebrate our one-two in Hungary, so I was able to chat to everyone there. I knew we would be running the revised rear suspension and gearbox for the first time at a race meeting; I was really looking forward to getting down to business.'

Life in Formula One is never that simple. Coulthard was limited to just nine of the permitted 23 laps on Friday morning, thanks to a problem with the hydraulics on his car. But, worse than that, he was perturbed to find that the balance of the FW17B was not as he would have hoped. Hill was much happier, but then he had the benefit of having run with the latest set-up at Silverstone. Coulthard began to think that Damon would carry that advantage with him throughout the weekend; David's hopes of taking pole began to recede, particularly after he had qualified second to Hill on the first day.

Saturday morning seemed little better as Coulthard continued to feel ill at ease with the handling of the car, a worry which was exacerbated by Hill's relaxed and confident demeanour. David decided he had nothing to lose by trying Damon's settings and then working from there. It was the correct move; the car was transformed.

'I was prepared to do anything to get pole,' stressed Coulthard. 'The car felt a lot better but I knew Damon would be difficult to beat during final qualifying. I would have to push very hard indeed, so hard that I knew I would either win pole or crash. You may think that every driver sets out with the intention of doing his utmost but there are various levels of how hard you are prepared to push. That Saturday at Estoril, I was prepared to go absolutely to the limit.'

He did – and took pole from Damon by just 0.368 seconds during the course of a spectacular 2.7-mile lap. Now Coulthard had to translate that advantage into the result he wanted so much. The only problem was that Damon would be running just as strongly, but with the championship as his first priority. Would David therefore be constrained by team orders and denied that elusive maiden victory? That had been the case at Estoril the previous year, when Coulthard had been asked to let Hill through. This time, however, Coulthard was the master of the track. So far.

Hill and Coulthard had a chat on race morning. It was agreed that if David was ahead, but holding up Damon, he would let Hill go through. On the other had, if David was quicker, then tough luck on Damon. It was a reasonable compromise, one which left Coulthard in no doubt about what he needed to do. It would be a repeat of the all-or-nothing exercise of final qualifying, except that, on this occasion, it would last for 71 laps rather than just one. It would be maximum effort for an hour and 40 minutes as opposed to a mere 80 seconds.

In actual fact, the drama would last for close to two hours although, at one point, Coulthard must have wondered if this race would ever get going. Carefully avoiding a repeat of Monza, David reached his grid position safely enough this time and made a clean start. Unfortunately, the same could not be said for Ukyo Katayama, as the Tyrrell driver somehow managed to tangle wheels with a Minardi before launching into a violent series of airborne spins and rolls and bouncing off the crash barrier, the wreckage landing upside-down on the track. Jock

Clear used the radio to give Coulthard the news that the race had been stopped.

As David came to a halt on the grid once more, and while waiting for the track to be cleared, he had time to return to worries about different matters which might affect his race. For instance it had been decided that despite the obvious performance advantage offered by the revised car, any gain would be useless if neither driver finished. There were worries over a gearbox bearing giving trouble and, with that in mind, it was decided to return to the original rear-end specification for the race.

'It was a proven package,' said David. 'That was comforting because we were at least going back to a car which we knew. On the other hand, I was nervous that we would lose the advantage gained over Benetton. Psychologically, it was a backward step. I had to keep up the momentum, particularly after deciding that we needed to stop three times during the race.

'There had been a lot of discussion during debriefing on Saturday concerning the number of stops we would make. I have to say that, at first, I was comfortable with doing just two. It was a case of the Scottish conservatism which says if you go for an extra stop then that's merely another chance to get it wrong in the pits. It's a problem to know what to do for the best and in the end it was clear that the fastest way from start to finish would be to be quick over each individual lap.'

The answer would be to make three stops because, more often than not, the car would be running with less fuel on board compared to the load he would carry if stopping only twice. Coulthard would also have the benefit of fresh tyres more often. But the key would be leading the race into the first corner. David had managed it first time round. Now he had to do it all over again.

'And that was another worry,' admitted Coulthard. 'To accelerate from standstill for another warm-up lap and start puts an extra load on the gearbox and clutch. That is a serious issue because F1 cars are designed to do one more lap than a race distance and that is all. The thought of putting the car through that stress becomes critical when you have been suffering from reliability problems.'

Coulthard put those fears behind him from the outset. He not only led into the first corner but set what would turn out to be the fastest lap of the race on just his second lap. Schumacher was second, with Hill third. The gap to the Benetton increased with each lap, from 1.2 seconds at the end of lap one to 5.7 seconds after ten laps. David looked smooth and unruffled. Inside the cockpit, however, there was all manner of serious activity.

'I was pushing very hard but I'm sure that was difficult to see from the outside because I like to remain smooth and tidy,' said Coulthard. 'There was always the fear that Schumacher might be stopping just twice, in which case I needed to build an even bigger advantage. I got to the point where I was putting everything into it, both physically and mentally, and on top of that there was the tension associated with the fact that I had been with a top team for twenty Grands Prix, I had a good car – and I hadn't won a race. There were so many emotions to deal with.

'Until I knew for certain that Michael was stopping three times, I had to presume that he was on a two-stop strategy, in which case he was going to beat me. I was trying to work out how I could give even more and I came to the conclusion that it was impossible.

'Estoril is a very tough circuit – bumps, very fast corners, undulations, heavy braking – and I reached the stage where I was trying so hard that I wasn't sure if I could breathe any more. Tension affects the way you are in the car – not necessarily the way you drive – but it has an effect on things such as breathing. It was not a case of desperation as such but one of realization that I was coming to the end of my time with Williams and I knew what I was capable of. But I had yet to prove it to the outside world. I simply had to do it now that I had a chance like this.'

As the first pit stops came and went, Coulthard faced

pressure of another kind. The leaders had already dealt with the back-markers but now they faced the reasonably quick mid-field runners; people such as Hakkinen, Barrichello and Frentzen, drivers who were fighting their own battles and would not be in such a hurry to move out of the way. Schumacher had the capacity to scythe through slower cars without a moment's hesitation. Coulthard would have to do the same, otherwise the Benetton would be on his tail in no time at all. The gap between the leaders did reduce, but only by a couple of tenths of a second. This was a massive test of Coulthard's judgement, determination and nerve. He came through it brilliantly.

Hill, meanwhile, was in all sorts of trouble. A change of plan in the early stages of the race had seen Damon switch from a three-stop strategy to a two in the mistaken belief that Schumacher was doing the same. By the time Hill realized the extent of his rival's game plan, it was too late. The extra time taken to add more fuel (to cope with just one more stop) meant Hill rejoined in the middle of traffic and lost nine seconds in the space of three laps as he struggled unsuccessfully to get past Jean Alesi just before the Ferrari, running with a light load, made its pit stop.

Hill actually led the race for five laps when the two- and three-stop tactics overlapped at around half distance. But once the final stops had been made, Coulthard was

■ ■

back in charge with Hill second and Schumacher, thanks to the benefit of fresh tyres after a recent stop, rushing forward to catch the second-place Williams.

Attention switched from the battle for the race to the fight for the championship. With Schumacher enjoying a 15-point lead Hill could not afford to finish behind his rival, but he was powerless to prevent the Benetton snatching second place with less than ten laps to go. Coulthard was safe enough, thanks to an 11-second lead. Even so, all manner of thoughts were rushing through his head.

'The last ten laps were possibly the hardest,' admitted David. 'I wasn't under a lot of pressure and I had time to worry about something going wrong. On the last lap, I didn't know what to do. I wanted to talk to the team but I didn't want to tempt fate. I saw a blur of Williams team colours cheering on the pit wall as I approached the finish line but I kept going flat out. I had a horrible thought that maybe I'd dreamt I'd seen the chequered flag, so I didn't slow down in case I had to do another lap.'

There was no such danger. David Coulthard had just become the first Scotsman to win a Grand Prix since Jackie Stewart's last victory before retirement in 1973. But, of more immediate importance, this was a just reward for David's mechanics, Stewart Prattley, Robbie Tyers, Gary Woodward and Dave Juniper, who had not savoured that unparalleled feeling of satisfaction all season.

■ ■

Whether by chance or design, Coulthard discovered there were no flights to Nice that evening. It was just as well, perhaps, since he was engulfed by the media outside the Williams motor-home. Inside, Damon Hill did his best to put a gloss on a championship which was slipping from his grasp, but which was not yet over. Then he grabbed his briefcase and dashed to the airport.

Following a lively dinner with Rothmans personnel, Coulthard joined his mechanics and several drivers at the Coconut nightclub in the nearby seaside town of Estoril, where he judged the Miss Coconut competition. In his column in the *Daily Telegraph* on Tuesday 26 September, Coulthard wrote: 'It [the competition] basically involved assessing a line-up of topless models. I wouldn't mention this in a family newspaper except that entrant Number 6 won – the same number as my car – which gave a nice symmetry to the weekend.'

The feeling of having come full circle was also shared in the Williams motor-home, where Paul and Frances Edwards toasted Coulthard's success. The chef and his wife had worked with David when they were all employed by the same Formula 3000 team a few years before. But the celebration was brief. In fact, if they were brutally honest, Paul and Frances, and their assistant chef, Hilary Weaver, were a touch annoyed that David had chosen to score his great victory at this particular Grand Prix. The

Williams motor-home crew, along with the rest of the paddock, were now in the thick of a race of their own.

By a bizarre arrangement of the calendar, the next race, the European Grand Prix, would be staged the following weekend, 1,500 miles away in Germany. The motor-homes and transporters had to be there by Wednesday. It was a tall order, but typical of the exceptional challenge motor-racing people had to face during the course of a season.

A relief driver had been flown to Portugal to assist on the journey, Edwards having carefully gone through the logistics of the double-header race meetings with Dickie Stanford. Before leaving England on the round trip, Edwards had stocked up with 60 cases of drink (including 20 cases of beer) and top-quality fillet steak and smoked salmon. The most important and expensive meal each day would be breakfast, a typical race weekend accounting for 80 lbs of bacon, 50 lbs of Lincolnshire pork sausages and 20 lbs of black pudding. Fruit, vegetables, bread and eggs would be purchased locally, not a problem in Estoril but slightly more difficult at the Nürburgring due to its comparatively remote location in the Eifel Mountains, 50 miles south of Cologne.

Once the motor-home has been manoeuvred into a position predetermined by Pasquale Lattunedu, the representative of the Formula One Constructors' Association,

it takes the crew approximately 26 hours to set up in the paddock. Jobs range from painting the garage in preparation for the arrival of the trucks to washing and polishing the motor-home, scrubbing and erecting the awnings and external temporary floors, arranging 40 chairs and tables, positioning palm trees (which are used for decorative purposes but do not travel well and need replacing every three races) and sorting out the kitchen accommodation.

When motor-homes first began to appear in the 1970s, their original purpose was to provide privacy for the team management, with facilities for the occasional cup of tea. The mechanics would eat in hotels and local restaurants, with the motor-home providing sandwiches – at a push. The increase in professionalism and the arrival of sponsors heaped further demands on the motor-home staff and Paul Edwards would no more consider attempting to use the cramped kitchen inside the motor-home than a mechanic would accept a stale croissant and coffee for breakfast.

The Williams hardware arrives in a separate truck which carries everything, including a catering-size kitchen sink. A six-burner oven, three fridges, two deep-freezes and temporary shelving and worktops complete the paraphernalia arranged under an extension to the

. . . .

awning at the rear of a motor-home which, in full comba-
tive order, is worth £500,000.

The dark blue Williams motor-home had reached the
Nürburgring at 4.30 p.m. on Tuesday, the journey from
Estoril having been interrupted only by a seven-hour rest
halt. Having literally made themselves at home, Edwards
and his crew provided a light lunch for the truck drivers
on Wednesday, with something slightly more substantial
the following day to cope with the arrival of team guests,
sponsors and one or two members of the press. Serious
business would begin on Friday.

The girls arose at 5.45 a.m., Paul stirring 45 minutes
later in time to have breakfast under way for the arrival
of the mechanics at 7.15 a.m. The engineers, public
relations and sponsorship staff, guests, media and drivers
appeared at various stages throughout the next hour and,
by the time the last fried egg had been turned, approximately 75 breakfasts had been served.

Frank Williams arrived mid-morning, not long after
Paul had set off on a shopping expedition and the girls
had begun pit duties by providing a constant supply of
cold drinks, tea, coffee and snacks for the garage. Then
they turned their attention to lunch.

Paul would have already received a list of Frank's
guests, including sponsors from Segafredo and Black
Tower. With friends of the drivers looking for somewhere

. . . .

to eat, the guest list might grow to 25, a typical three-course lunch consisting of tortellini, navarin of lamb with vegetables and garlic Lyonnaise potatoes, followed by peach and kiwi tart.

Once activity on the track has finished for the day, the Williams motor-home area is invariably a popular spot for afternoon tea, thanks to the home-made cakes and sponges, just a small part of a repertoire gathered by Hilary and Frances in divergent locations and branches of the catering trade. Hilary Weaver, a former head chef in a hotel on the Isle of Skye, went from one extreme to the other when she swapped the calm of the Scottish Islands for the hurly-burly of world travel. Frances was a maternity nurse when she met her future husband in London.

It was inevitable that Paul should end up in his present role since he had travelled widely, particularly when training as a chef on the *Queen Elizabeth* and the *Queen Mary* ocean liners before working in Barbados for a period and then running a delicatessen with Frances in Kensington. A former British hill-climb champion, Paul began to mix business with pleasure when asked by a small sports car team to provide refreshments at Le Mans, a diversion that would lead to the formation of a catering company which not only deals with Formula One but also the Williams Touring Car team, the Paul Stewart Racing team in

Formula 3000, and all hospitality at the Williams Conference Centre in Didcot.

Edwards charges a flat fee per race ('Williams are brilliant payers,' says Paul. 'You receive your cheque within ten days') and it is up to him to ensure that he has covered all eventualities – such as suddenly discovering that he will have to provide dinner for 40 on the Friday evening at the Nurburgring as the mechanics settled into an unexpectedly long night working on the revised gearbox and rear suspension.

After the promise shown during practice in Estoril, it was decided to race the modified cars for the first time, but that entailed extra checking and detailed refinements. The intensive effort was worth it as Coulthard took his third pole position in succession, to level the season score at seven each for the fastest Williams driver during qualifying. Hill was not far behind, with Schumacher having edged closer to the Williams pair despite the track being damp in places during final qualifying. The Williams FW17B had the edge but no one was discounting Schumacher, particularly in front of a passionate home crowd.

The world championship battle between Hill and Schumacher apart, there was only one major talking point around the tables outside the Williams motor-home. The entire paddock had been caught on the hop by the news, released the previous Tuesday, that Eddie Irvine would be leaving Jordan to join Schumacher at Ferrari in 1996. If that was the best-kept secret, then the worst was Coulthard's move to McLaren, the announcement on the Sunday morning in Germany barely causing a ripple. In any case, David was concerned about more immediate matters such as winning this race and, if he could, helping Damon to close the 17-point gap to Schumacher.

The matter would not arise since Coulthard would never really look like winning. In an extraordinary repeat of Monza, David spun off while on his way to the grid. 'There was a lot of water about and, coming through the fast chicane, the car got sideways,' said Coulthard. 'I was so surprised that I didn't even dip the clutch and the engine stalled. I got on the radio to Jock and told him what had happened. He didn't believe me at first . . .'

The spare car was set up for Hill but the team made a very quick change to the pedals, belts and seat in time to have Coulthard take his place on pole. That was to be a fitting start to a race made dramatic mainly by atrocious weather. Drivers could not decide whether to risk switching to slicks in the hope that it would dry. Ferrari made the gamble and it almost paid off, thanks to a typically courageous and flamboyant drive by Jean Alesi. The main interest, however, was in the latest round of the fight between Schumacher and Hill.

Damon made a bad start (off line and on the wettest

side of the grid) but he chased Schumacher relentlessly, managed to get by, only to throw away his advantage two corners later by running wide. Hill's next attempt (at the same corner as before) almost ended in disaster as Schumacher robustly defended his place and Hill touched the back of the Benetton. There was no damage done but the same could not be said a few laps later and at the same corner, when Hill's desperate attempt to pass Alesi ended in tears as Hill's nose wing was broken. The collision had also damaged his steering and that would contribute to a spin, followed by a meeting with the barrier which would be painful in every sense. The moment the Williams went in, sideways on and very fast, Damon knew his championship was more or less over.

Schumacher, seeing that Hill was out, knew he had 17 points in the bank and that it was worth putting a risky move on Alesi in order to take the lead. In typical style, Schumacher allowed Alesi the option of either giving way or crashing. They briefly interlocked wheels and Alesi had no complaint about it afterwards, mainly because he had just suffered the same treatment he had meted out to Hill, but with less disastrous consequences for the challenger.

Hill had no complaints either. As Schumacher completed his victorious slowing down lap before a rapturous audience, Damon stepped from behind the barrier and publicly applauded his rival. It was a generous move which Schumacher appreciated. Coulthard had finished third, a small player on the sidelines of such extrovert performances by the men with whom he shared the rostrum. The Williams team members, after all their strenuous efforts, were nonplussed.

So, too, was Damon. As he gingerly climbed the front steps of the motor-home and sat down on the leather settee, the effect of having his legs thrown violently together in the impact with the barrier was making itself known. It would later be discovered that Hill had suffered a hairline fracture in his lower right leg but, in the meantime, that pain was being subjugated by mental agony as he tried to work out what had gone wrong.

Once again, he had been forced to deal with aggressive tactics which went beyond the acceptable standards he had been brought up to respect. As he sipped a cup of tea, it was clear that the sporting win-at-all-costs attitude of the Nineties was causing turmoil within him. More to the point, the fact that these moves were *permitted* was perhaps of greater concern than the tactics themselves. While Paul Edwards and his crew bustled back and forth to begin the packing away, Hill sat quietly, unsure what to think, what to do next.

One of the best races of the season would be encapsulated not long afterwards in the tunnel running beneath the main straight. Schumacher, beaming and striding briskly, led a jostling mob of television crews and reporters as he made his way from the press centre to the pits where, still dressed in his champagne-soaked overalls, he was about to share his pleasure with the Benetton team for the first time.

Barely 20 minutes later, Hill came through the tunnel in the opposite direction. Changed out of his overalls and wrapped against the cold in a Rothmans anorak, Damon was limping quite severely now. Accompanied only by a friend, Hill cut a lonely figure in the cavernous emptiness of the tunnel. He had given his best. But it had not been good enough.

CHAPTER EIGHT

DOWN HILL
IN JAPAN

PACIFIC AND JAPAN

Two days after the European Grand Prix, Frank Williams was airborne once more, his beige and brown Falcon 50 jet heading for Le Mans in France. The mission – a goodwill visit to La Filière, a racing drivers' school run by Elf Oil – had little to do with Formula One, but Frank's thoughts continued to be occupied by the calamitous events on the previous Sunday. He covered his disappointment with typical sang-froid.

During the 55-minute return flight to Oxford airport, Frank was glowing in his praise for Elf's efforts to nurture future champions – which was ironic considering Williams now had to admit that, for the second year running, his team could not boast a world champion of its own. Schumacher and Benetton had destroyed the Williams attack;

the final three races in Japan and Australia would be more or less a formality when it came to totting up drivers' championship points.

The flight to Japan would be a long haul for Frank but at least the private jet would make the journey reasonably easy and allow for the disability brought about by a road accident in 1986. When his hire car rolled into a field in the south of France, the impact broke a vertebra high in Williams's back and left him a tetraplegic. It is a massive handicap which Frank dismisses with the same absence of self-pity which he applies to the cause of the accident in the first place. 'I was going too fast and cocked it up,' he says with disarming candour. Then he flashes his winning smile and steers the conversation on to other matters.

'So, who's going to win in Aida?' he asked, knowing full well that the only answer he was interested in – and always had been – was the next victory for Williams Grand Prix Engineering.

The following day, Damon Hill was entertaining similar thoughts during a mid-week test session at Imola in Italy; Schumacher needed just three more points but that would not stop Hill trying to win and make up, in small part, for the dissatisfaction he felt after the most recent races. Damon then returned to Dublin for an unsuitably short break with his wife Georgie and his three children before catching a flight to Japan on the Sunday evening, exactly a week before the Pacific Grand Prix was due to be held at Aida.

Hill's first few days in Japan were spent in the sprawling city of Osaka, as good a place as any to move around with anonymity while adjusting to the eight-hour time difference. Europeans can never become accustomed to the Japanese diet during such a brief visit. Damon took the opportunity for a last bash at western cuisine by visiting the Hard Rock Café, a rowdy, bustling place where the disc-jockey, in his best effort at English, implored customers to come back in a week's time for the 'Har Lock Crafé Harroween Plarty'. Hill was about to encounter fireworks of his own at Aida and Suzuka.

After three days of swimming and the occasional saunter around the city, it was time to take the bullet train to Okayama. There, he collected a hire car and drove to Yunogo, the small town in a valley where his hotel was located, about a 30-minute drive from the circuit in the pine-clad hills above. By the time Damon arrived at the track on the Thursday afternoon, the preparations in the Williams garage were more or less complete.

The mechanics had also left London on the Sunday, a lengthy coach trip completing the 18-hour journey to this remote corner. With entertainment being thin on the ground, the members of various teams amused themselves out of hours by playing football on the starting grid, reading, listening to portable music centres or renewing acquaintances with Monopoly and other long-forgotten board games.

There was time for worthy gestures and the return of favours. Les Jones, a mechanic on Hill's car, and Gary Woodward (now fully recovered from the injury received in the swimming pool in Montreal) borrowed a barbecue from the Jordan team and gave Paul, Frances and Hilary a night off by cooking dinner for the catering staff and the rest of the team.

That part of the evening was a success but a minor disaster occurred later on when a technician fell off a roller-blade and broke his leg. The incident, which called for the injured party to be flown home and a replacement engineer dispatched immediately, had absolutely nothing to do with a lethal brand of liquid refreshment which had been produced, purely for medicinal purposes of course, in order to help those with jet-lag get some sleep.

Such emergencies concerning the engine manufacturer were outside the remit of the chief mechanic, Carl Gaden. His interests were focused on the well-being of the Williams mechanics, four of whom were new to long-distance travel and its potentially debilitating side-effects. Carl had been around long enough to know what to expect, his experience in Formula One stretching back several years to an association with the Goodyear Tyre and Rubber Company and then the Arrows team.

Carl joined Williams in 1988, when he worked on the test team before moving on to the race team 12 months later. Following the usual progression, he was allocated at first to the spare car and then promoted to one of the race cars; in this instance, the Williams driven by Thierry Boutsen.

Gaden continued to be part of the threesome working with the Belgian driver in 1990 and, when Boutsen left at the end of the season, Carl found himself part of Nigel Mansell's crew on the Englishman's return to Williams in 1991. Since then, Gaden had worked with Alain Prost, Ayrton Senna, David Coulthard and Mansell again during his brief reappearances with Williams in 1994 as the team tried to regroup in the terrible aftermath of Senna's death.

Gaden had spent some of that time working as a Number 1 mechanic. Such a wide range of experience moved his name to the head of the list of prospective candidates when Dickie Stanford was promoted from the role of chief mechanic to team manager at the beginning of 1995. Gaden accepted the advancement in the knowledge that it could cause some ill-feeling among the lads with whom he had worked, shoulder to shoulder, during the previous few years.

'I was a bit apprehensive at first,' said Carl. 'But Dickie

∎∎

■ ■

has been really good. If he thinks I have done something wrong, we'll talk it through rather than have him wading in with criticism. Mechanics have their various ways of doing things and some of the lads probably thought one or two of my ideas were wrong; I would probably have felt the same. But I had to look at the wider picture rather than just the job in hand. The chief mechanic has to think about the team as a whole and about the actual races. Some of the ideas you put forward seem wrong in the short term but these modifications to the car and changes in the way of working are being incorporated in the interests of reliability.

'On top of all that, you have to make sure that everything runs smoothly. Having double-header races in Europe, followed by two a week apart in Japan, is a bit of a nightmare. Certainly, the race at the Nürburgring was one of the worst weekends I can remember.'

Carl was referring not so much to the result, but to the fact that he had reached bed at 3 a.m. on the Friday night – and that was a luxury compared with what was to follow. The decision to race the latest rear suspension and gearbox brought with it a lot of extra work and detail refinement, with revised parts being sent from the factory during the course of the weekend. Gaden had gone back to the hotel on the Saturday evening, gathered his things, returned to the track and worked right through. The gen-

■ ■

erator in the Williams truck had been fired up as usual on the Saturday morning and it would remain running until just before the trucks left the paddock on Sunday night. Gaden and the mechanics could only hope the Pacific Grand Prix would not be such a punishing event. It was the last thing they needed. The season, by this stage, seemed never-ending.

Everything went according to plan, Coulthard taking pole position for the fourth race in succession, with Hill starting from the outside of the front row. The chief mechanic kept his usual watching brief, checking the overview rather than becoming embroiled in the detailed spanner work. Gaden could read the minds of his men and was ready to lend a hand in awkward moments without having to be asked. He would explain the latest developments and ensure that new parts were fitted in the manner intended by Patrick Head and Adrian Newey. And the good thing was that any advantageous modifications would be given to both drivers rather than just the Number 1, as is the way with some teams.

'That's the great thing about Williams,' said Carl. 'It's the team that matters most. Everyone in the garage knows that no one has an advantage over anyone else. Mechanics like to think that their particular car is the best in the garage. There is nothing worse than working on a car and knowing that the other car is getting all the latest bits. It's

■■■■■■■■■■■■■■■■■■■■■■■■■■■■■■■■■■■

good for the team as a whole when both cars are the same and everyone has the same opportunity to win. Of course you want the team to win but each mechanic has a special affinity with his car and his driver. If the other car wins, then of course you'll congratulate your mates. But there is nothing better – nothing at all – when it's your car which wins the race. That's a bit special.'

So, who would experience that special feeling in Aida? The crew from Coulthard's winning car in Portugal? Or Bob Davis, Les Jones, Paul West and Matthew White, the mechanics responsible for Hill's car? Of course, there was always the possibility that Robbie Campbell, Alan Broadhead and Chris Hyatt could have the unexpected pleasure if the spare car was pressed into action for the race. But the basic truth was that the team needed a decent result, since with 14 races run, Benetton had scored nine victories to just four for Williams. David or Damon; it mattered little which of the two it was.

For the first 15 laps, it seemed certain that the Pacific Grand Prix was going the way of Coulthard. A clean start for the Scotsman had been helped considerably by Jean Alesi slotting into second place when the Ferrari driver made the most of a minor squabble as Hill and Schumacher disputed the right of passage through the first corner.

With the Ferrari being comparatively slow on a circuit

■■■■■■■■■■■■■■■■■■■■■■■■■■■■■■■■■■■

where overtaking is very difficult, Coulthard had been allowed to pull out a 12-second lead in just 14 laps. If anything, it was too good because such an unexpected advantage lulled Coulthard into a false sense of security and tempted him to believe that he could get away with two pit stops instead of three – his original intention. The change of plan – entirely Coulthard's decision – would cost him the race.

Hill, meanwhile, was hacking through painfully familiar ground as he tried to get past the Ferrari while, at the same time, defending his third place from the attentions of Schumacher. With Alesi vigorously guarding his position, and the memory of the Nürburgring burned into the subconscious, Hill began to rely increasingly on the fast-approaching first pit stop as the only means of getting ahead. Indeed, the refuelling stop would bring a change to the pattern of the race, but not in the direction Hill had hoped.

By chance, all three cars came into the pit lane together. Unfortunately for Hill, the Ferrari pit was placed before the Williams garage, which meant Hill had to slow down and then accelerate briefly in order to avoid Alesi as he entered his pit. But the biggest disaster was to occur when the refuelling hose would not connect to the Williams. The equipment is so sensitive that if the hose does not make perfect contact at the first attempt, a locking

mechanism will prevent completion of the coupling, a
safety feature which can only be overcome by removing
the hose and quickly resetting the valve. Hill was unaware
of the problem until, to his utter dismay, he saw Schumacher and then Alesi accelerate away while the Williams
remained stationary.

By the time the connection had been made and the
fuel added, six seconds had been lost. Worse still, that
delay meant Hill rejoined in the midst of a squabbling
bunch of mid-field runners. The Benetton team had been
so quick that Schumacher was now second and Hill's
sequence of problems had been so bad that, within just
seven laps, Schumacher was 20 seconds ahead. Hill had
no hope of recovering.

Coulthard was still in the lead, of course, but his advantage was about to disappear after his first pit stop, courtesy
of stubborn behaviour as Heinz-Harald Frentzen refused
to give way while being lapped. The five laps spent stuck
behind the Sauber cost Coulthard eight seconds and
contributed to Schumacher taking the lead as the
sequence of pit stops unfolded. After his final stop, Schumacher rejoined just in front of Coulthard. And pulled
away. Victory number eight for Schumacher – and
impressive confirmation of his world championship.

Once again, the Williams team was in a state of shock.
Victory appeared to have been theirs for the taking and

yet Benetton had snatched it away. Coulthard had finished second, Hill third. In and around the grey-painted temporary offices lining the rear edge of the paddock, the moods varied hugely. The Benetton engineers and technicians stood around outside, smoking, drinking and enjoying the moment. At the end of the row, the blinds remained drawn on the window of the Williams office. Inside, sitting around a rectangular table, Coulthard and Hill dissected their respective races with their engineers and Patrick Head. As if to rub it in, the race was being replayed on the television screen hanging from a corner of the room. Frank Williams had long since departed this tortured scene.

Meanwhile, back in England, no mercy was being shown. In an unprecedented attack in motor sports terms, the general sports writers of the British national daily newspapers were tearing Hill apart. From positions of little personal knowledge but considerable influence, the armchair experts castigated Damon for being a whinger and a poor loser. It was not necessarily a view which the regular Formula One correspondents supported – but that didn't sell newspapers. It was a devastating attack which Hill did his best to ignore while on a trip to Tokyo.

The capital city of Japan did at least provide plenty of diversions, as David Coulthard and Andrea Murray discovered when the mischievous influences of Gerhard

Berger took them to a night club which, to David's discomfort, left little to the imagination. By the following Thursday, the Formula One circus had begun to gather at Suzuka, a far more acceptable venue than the remote Aida.

Pete Boutwood, a close friend of Damon, had flown to Japan to provide some support and company. The pair of them walked the circuit, Boutwood understanding for the first time the full depth of Suzuka's magnificent challenge. He also appreciated even more the quality of Hill's victory on this track 12 months earlier, when he had beaten Schumacher under the most difficult conditions imaginable as rain made the circuit even more treacherous than usual.

The hope was that Damon would be able to repeat that performance this weekend. In fact, it was a must if Williams was to prevent Benetton from taking the Constructors' Championship as well as the drivers' title. The chances, however, seemed slim as Hill, tense and preoccupied, faced the press for his pre-race briefing.

It wasn't a press conference as such, more an informal gathering around a fold-away table outside the Williams office in the paddock. Everyone was aware of the abuse which had been dished out at home but the subject was not raised. Hill spoke in generalities.

'I know I've had problems . . . last week was a bit of a disaster but there's no reason why I can't win this race . . .

■■■

I've won it before . . . The team is behind me . . . It's been a long and difficult season . . . We've got a very good car . . . We have every faith . . .'

Damon couldn't wait to be finished. When he stood up and made a swift departure, none of those present held out much hope for the win he so desperately needed. This was the haunted shadow of the Damon Hill the journalists had come to know and respect. He appeared to be a beaten man, even before the weekend had started.

Such subtleties were not yet evident to Carl Gaden and his mechanics as they made themselves at home in the garage at the top of the pit lane. A five-hour coach journey from Aida on the Monday had delivered the lads to Suzuka at 6 p.m. By 6.30 p.m., they were hard at work.

Part of the setting up would include the unpacking and installing of three telemetry screens at the back of the garage. Seated before them throughout practice and the race would be Simon Scoins, Ian Pearce and Grant Tuff as they monitored the performance of each car in minute detail.

Grant Tuff had joined Williams at the beginning of the season to fulfil the newly created role of sifting through the mountain of detail produced by the telemetry. The data logging process called for Tuff to download information from the cars when they were stationary in the pits. That had its obvious limitations but a deal between

■■■

▪▪▪▪▪▪▪▪▪▪▪▪▪▪▪▪▪▪▪▪▪▪▪▪▪▪▪▪▪▪▪▪▪▪▪

Williams and Telxon, a world leader in data capture and wireless communication technology, would allow the transmission of minute detail while the car was on the move. This sophisticated system was due to come on stream in 1996. In the meantime, Tuff and his colleagues would continue to rely on the tried and trusted method and it would not require a genius to work out that Williams were in a spot of bother.

Hill and Coulthard struggled to find a reasonable set-up on their cars but there appeared to be nothing too seriously wrong when Hill claimed provisional pole position with two minutes of qualifying remaining on Friday. Then came the dreaded warning in the dying seconds of the session as Schumacher turned in a lap which was 0.6 seconds quicker. Coulthard, on his first visit to the Suzuka track, was sixth fastest.

Schumacher did it again with just four seconds of final qualifying remaining. This time, however, his quick lap rubbed salt in a deepening Williams wound as neither Damon nor David were able to improve, Damon slipping back to fourth place. Clearly, Williams had gone in the wrong direction concerning the set-up on their cars.

Hill stayed in the team's small office with Patrick Head and David Brown until 8 p.m. as they discussed and debated every option. The venetian blinds remained shut tight, particularly on the window opening on to the world

▪▪▪▪▪▪▪▪▪▪▪▪▪▪▪▪▪▪▪▪▪▪▪▪▪▪▪▪▪▪▪▪▪▪▪

▪▪▪▪▪▪▪▪▪▪▪▪▪▪▪▪▪▪▪▪▪▪▪▪▪▪▪▪▪▪▪▪▪▪▪

outside the paddock where race fans would wait patiently all day for the slightest glimpse of their heroes. Using a scooter and unmarked crash helmet, Damon made his escape from the paddock and ran the gauntlet of the enthusiastic but politely insistent fans. He had dinner with Pete Boutwood and Jon Nicholson in a nearby Italian restaurant. Then it was a sprint back to the hotel and bed by 10.30 p.m. At that moment, the mechanics were finishing their work in the garage. It was a reasonably early night all round; that was the only good thing which would happen during the course of the next 24 hours.

Hill awoke to the sound of rain lashing the concrete outside the Suzuka Circuit Hotel. It brought mixed feelings. No driver likes racing in the rain but it would level out the performance of the cars, since any advantage Benetton might have would not work to the full in the wet. The emphasis would switch to the skill of the driver.

Hill jumped on his scooter and then walked briskly to the Williams office, where he checked technical details with David Brown before moving into the temporary kitchen established by Paul Edwards in the office next door. A bowl of porridge, followed by tea and a chocolate croissant, set Hill up for the morning's work. He was keen to get going.

The warm-up began at 8.30 a.m. The track was wet and, straight away, Hill was on the pace. It was a busy

▪▪▪▪▪▪▪▪▪▪▪▪▪▪▪▪▪▪▪▪▪▪▪▪▪▪▪▪▪▪▪▪▪▪

■ ■

scene as Damon switched between his usual car and the spare chassis which, of course, would be used for the first time on race day. The mechanics, wearing sweaters as protection against the damp, early-morning chill, moved quickly. Hardly a word was spoken, signals and nods providing the choreography. Sponsorship representatives from Sanyo, ill-at-ease in the midst of such controlled bustle, stepped this way and that in an effort not to intrude.

Frank Williams, positioned in front of a television screen and monitors, stared intently at the constantly changing information. For once this weekend, the final lap times would make good reading; Hill was fastest with Coulthard third. In between them, the inevitable presence of Michael Schumacher. 'Yes,' agreed Damon, 'I don't like the wet but I have to be honest and say, with the way we've been going, it represents our best chance today.' Predictably, then, the rain stopped shortly before the race was due to start.

The dilemma was to decide what the weather would do during the next two hours. The forecast said there was a 60 per cent chance of rain. Indeed, the air still felt damp. But the skies were reasonably clear and the wind had dropped. It seemed a safe bet to assume that the track would dry sooner rather than later. The popular choice would be to start on rain tyres but with the cars set up

■ ■

for dry conditions. It was the most suitable compromise. However, because of the trouble experienced during practice, Williams had to explore other routes and employ educated guesswork when it came to establishing exactly what the best dry-weather set-up should be.

'I was effectively starting the race not knowing what to expect,' said Hill. 'Initially, it turned out rather well, except for the fact that I was stuck behind Mika Hakkinen, who had qualified his McLaren ahead of me. That cost me a lot of time in the opening laps but, thanks to some great teamwork in the pits, I was able to get ahead of the McLaren. Then Jean Alesi came steaming up behind me.

'Alesi was absolutely flying and I wasn't quite sure what had happened because he had started ahead of me on the grid and I hadn't overtaken the Ferrari. After the race, when I watched the video, I couldn't believe it when I saw that he had spun off at one point and he had also been into the pits for a ten-second stop-go penalty for jumping the start. And yet, after all of that, he was catching me hand over fist!

'Of course, what had happened was that he was furious about the penalty. He was really pumped up and preparing himself to have a go at me under-braking for the chicane. So I took a tight line and braked late. But Alesi was on a mission and there was no holding him back as he came round the outside. Then he set after Schumacher and was

■■■■■■■■■■■■■■■■■■■■■■■■■■■■■■■■■■■■■■

taking chunks out of Michael's lead when the Ferrari blew up. Now I was second once more and thinking maybe I could make inroads on the 20-second gap to the Benetton.'

That, in fact, would turn out to be wishful thinking. If Hill thought the weekend had been difficult up to this point, then the events which were to follow would make the previous occurrences a minor inconvenience.

The second round of pit stops, brilliantly executed once more by Williams, had allowed Damon to close the gap on Schumacher to 13 seconds. Then, on lap 36, while braking for the hairpin at the far end of the circuit, the Williams ploughed straight on and hit the outside kerb a mighty thump before bouncing on to the gravel run-off area. Fearing there might have been damage to the nose, Damon called at the pits once more for a replacement, rejoining in fifth place.

That became fourth on lap 40, which was both good news and bad news since the promotion had come at the expense of his team-mate, Coulthard having fallen victim to the same corner. The Williams drivers were not alone, at least two others spinning off a track made treacherous by a light shower of rain and a deposit of oil, possibly from the Forti-Ford which had pulled off at the exit of the hairpin. David had managed to rejoin after bouncing across the run-off area, but as he braked for the next

■■■■■■■■■■■■■■■■■■■■■■■■■■■■■■■■■■■■■■

corner gravel shot out of every lower orifice on the car, got under his tyres and spun the Williams into the tyre wall, this time for good.

Frank Williams, watching as usual from his position in front of the television monitor, had barely got over the dissatisfaction of seeing Coulthard lose second place when the cameras honed in on the final insult; there was Hill, stuck fast in the gravel on the outside of the very corner where he had gone off before. At that precise moment, Frank Williams knew he had lost the Constructors' Championship for the first time in four years. His grim expression never changed. To say he was disappointed would not make a start on it.

Damon took shelter in a nearby marshals' post and watched Schumacher stroke home to his ninth win of the season. Then he hitched a lift back to the pits and braced himself for an interview with Patrick Head, not the first stern discussion between these two during the course of a stormy weekend. After that, Hill was called before the race stewards, who fined him $10,000 for speeding in the pit lane, the second such offence committed by Hill this season.

Was there no end to this misery? Hill appeared stunned by the time he reached the Rothmans office, where he was handed a restorative glass of schnapps. It eased the pain in the short term but did little for the overwhelming sense of failure pervading the entire team.

Williams had lost good and proper and the desperate disappointment was reflected in the garage as Carl Gaden and his mechanics quietly went about the packing process, each item seemingly weighing twice as much as normal as weariness replaced the long-since departed flush of adrenalin. By the time the mechanics had repaired to the bar for a drink, Frank Williams was already airborne once more.

CHAPTER NINE

IT'S A FUNNY
OLD GAME

AUSTRALIA

Sixteen races down, one to go. At this stage, the season begins to drag, particularly when the championships have been settled. The only consolation is that the two-week gap between the final races allows time for a brief holiday.

Ann Bradshaw went to Bali for a week. Apart from two days spent at an Indycar race in New Hampshire in August, this was to be the only break she would get between the start of the season the previous March and the final round in Australia on 12 November. Even then, there would be no total escape from work.

At a restaurant one evening, a handful of Japanese race fans recognized Bradshaw and tried to communicate their enthusiasm for Williams and all things connected with

Grand Prix racing. The polite disruption was no surprise since Ann Bradshaw, the team member frequently seen on television holding an umbrella over Damon Hill as he sits on the starting grid, is the attractive public face of Williams Grand Prix Engineering. It is an appropriate role because Bradshaw is the press officer concerning all activities on the race track.

Ann's counterpart at Williams HQ is Jane Gorard. Jane handles public relations involving everything to do with the team away from the track: matters such as visits to the factory, the lifestyle of the drivers, media links with sponsors' companies, manufacturing products as diverse as sun glasses and mechanical diggers. As the season entered its final phase, Jane continued to run the office in Didcot while Ann braced herself for a busy few days in Adelaide, starting from the moment she landed in South Australia on Tuesday morning.

Channel Nine held the television rights to the Australian Grand Prix, thus giving them exclusive access to everything within the race track. Channels Seven and Ten were effectively locked out, leaving the competition to make the most of the team personalities when they were away from the circuit. It was Ann Bradshaw's job to help out by arranging interviews with anyone from the team who was prepared to stand still for a couple of minutes and speak to camera. Since the drivers were not due to arrive until later the next day, it was a difficult task feeding the media's insatiable appetite for stories.

Ann also had to organize a dinner for the team and arrange parting gifts for two of its members. David Brown, Hill's engineer, was due to join McLaren and this would be the last race for Robbie Campbell, the mechanic in charge of the spare car. Two hip flasks, suitably engraved, were made ready for the pleasantly informal dinner on Wednesday night. This time, the mechanics had time on their side, even though the cars had to be stripped down and prepared as if the pit garage in Adelaide was the factory at Didcot. Jim Barker, in charge of transmission sub-assembly, had an important role here, particularly as the notoriously bumpy street circuit would seek out any weaknesses in the gearbox.

The arrival of the drivers had sparked furious activity on Thursday as the cameras and journalists homed in. Bradshaw's most pressing task was to help out Clive James, who was in the process of making a documentary. The Australian broadcaster had asked to have Damon Hill and Michael Schumacher cooperate by being interviewed jointly. Both drivers readily agreed and, at a stroke, dispelled one of the scurrilous tales being propagated by certain sections of the British media, divisive and critical stories which Ann did her best to hide from Damon's eyes, at least until the final race was over.

There were further interruptions to Damon's preparations at the track when he was called on to speak to
Channel Nine and representatives of Renault's television
company. Then it was a press conference for both drivers
in the media centre, followed by phone calls by Ann to
arrange a dinner venue where David Coulthard would say
a formal farewell to the Renault technicians before the
Scotsman drove his last race for Williams and moved on
to McLaren.

David's future employers made the headlines during
the first qualifying session the following day when Mika
Hakkinen crashed heavily and was taken to hospital in a
coma. The news of the McLaren driver's grave condition
spread quickly.

Ann Bradshaw had to focus on the accident, without
raising too much alarm, during the course of her regular
Daily Telegraph post-practice phone-line bulletin. After
reading a prepared script to a recording machine in
London, further telephone work would follow as Britain,
ten and a half hours behind Adelaide, awoke to the worrying news. Among others, Ann talked to the breakfast programme on Fox FM, the local radio station serving the
area around the Williams headquarters.

There had also been interviews to arrange with Hill
for Channel Nine, and then Mark Fogarty, a motoring
journalist. Clive James wanted to talk to Coulthard's girl-

friend, Andrea Murray; guests of Rothmans needed to be updated, and there was a press release to be prepared for distribution in two languages in the media centre. At least there was some good news, Hill had taken provisional pole position; but, against the background of Hakkinen's crash, that seemed irrelevant.

The accident dominated conversation at a Rothmans evening cocktail party, Ann rounding up both drivers to make sure they did their bit by being nice to people at the function in the Terrace Hotel. That done, Damon went off for a private dinner with the former motorcycle champion Barry Sheene, and David accompanied Ann to the next official engagement, a Renault dinner at Ayers House, the restaurant the team had used two nights previously. Ironically, Ayers House is situated across the road from the Royal Adelaide Hospital. It was impossible not to glance at the sprawling buildings and offer a silent prayer for the racing driver fighting for his life inside.

It was with some trepidation that Ann Bradshaw waited for her radio alarm at 6.30 the following morning. The news was very encouraging. Hakkinen's condition had improved considerably; doctors were cautiously optimistic.

The pit lane set to work with a lighter heart, Hill getting down to business once more by setting fastest time in the morning practice session. Hard at work, too, was Clive

■ ■

James's camera crew, the sound man's furry microphone causing some consternation by being poked into places it had no right to be. It was Ann's job to pour oil on troubled waters and placate those team members who felt their private conversations had been violated. Come final qualifying, the film crew had been briefed on their limitations when operating within the already crowded confines of the garage.

This was definitely the place to be; the Williams drivers were first and second quickest, Damon Hill taking pole position. Now it was Ann's turn to go into action at the double.

Since they had been the fastest, both drivers were taken straight to the front of the garage for the traditional interviews with the host broadcaster, in this case, Channel Nine. Then a chat with Clive James before being whisked upstairs to the media centre and a press conference for the fastest three drivers. This, at least, was a blessing for Ann Bradshaw, since it gave her an adequate opportunity to gather quotes for the afternoon press bulletin and, of course, the phone-line transmission and broadcasts which were due to follow later in the day.

Once the drivers had been safely delivered back to the garage for the debrief with their engineers, Ann made her way to another temporary office where she would start

■ ■

typing the press release in readiness for translation into French before photocopying.

Back upstairs once more, Ann weaved her way through the long lines of tables, distributing the releases as the media pounded out their stories. Throughout her progress, Bradshaw's cheery and sometimes cheeky remarks brought welcome levity to a business which can frequently take itself too seriously. Besides, the mood in the press room was good, since the latest bulletin from the hospital had brought more encouraging news concerning Mika Hakkinen.

As this would be the last race of the season, the drivers would be inundated with requests for autographs, mainly from team members and sponsors to serve as a memento of their year together. Bradshaw had to bear the brunt of the drivers' frustration, particularly when she presented Hill with a box filled with photographs, hats, t-shirts and helmet visors, all of which had to be signed with enough care and attention to give the recipient the feeling that this was the only autograph which had been produced all day.

In fact, it would take almost all of Saturday before Ann could persuade Damon to work his way through the box. He finished at 8 p.m., Ann leaving soon afterwards for her only private dinner of the weekend. And this would have to be enjoyed in strict moderation since her presence was required for the annual team photograph, to be taken in the pit lane at around 8 a.m.

The time was approximate thanks to the photographers having to dash from one garage to the next as they tried to make the most of this end-of-season gathering of each team. As Bradshaw was to discover, it was difficult to marshal the full crew, particularly the drivers, at precisely the right moment. Then it was time for breakfast, Paul Edwards taking care to include Ann Bradshaw's favourite cereal, Kelloggs Common Sense, in his box of accessories.

Throughout the morning, the end-of-term feeling in the paddock gathered strength as addresses were exchanged and informal presentations made to team members who were moving on, either to a rival or away from the sport altogether. Paradoxically, it was for this very reason that the atmosphere within the Williams garage continued to have a definite edge to it.

There were points to prove in Adelaide: Coulthard very keen to win his last race for the team; David Brown just as anxious to leave Williams and Damon Hill on a victorious note; both Brown and Jock Clear, having worked all weekend off their own bat in the absence of Patrick Head and Adrian Newey, hoping to show that they could cope by themselves. And Hill himself was quietly determined to make amends for recent disappointments by finishing the season with his first win since Hungary, almost three months before.

As the tension gathered, Bradshaw had to deal with a request from a Reuters photographer who wanted one of the special garage passes issued by the team in order to restrict the numbers of non-essential people. Ann had 12 such passes available and these had already been allocated to magazines such as *Vogue Australia*, working on a feature on the team. The photographer's plea that his rival from Associated Press had been given exclusive access cut no ice, Bradshaw explaining that AP had the foresight to request a garage pass a few weeks in advance.

It was almost a relief for Ann when the time came to walk to the grid and do her bit with the umbrella. In fact, her duties stretched to assisting Damon with the sticky tape which secured his radio-receivers-cum-ear plugs in place, and then looking after his drinking bottle once the final swig had been taken and the flameproof balaclava and crash helmet pulled into place. After the cars had left the grid for their final parade lap, Ann joined the flow of mechanics and officials walking briskly towards an opening in the pit wall. Now followed the bit which people in the grandstand opposite had paid more than £100 to see. Ann Bradshaw couldn't bear to look.

'I stand in the garage, just behind Frank [Williams],' she explained. 'Frank is watching the television picture

■■■

and the two timing monitors but I position myself so that I can't see the TV. My theory is that if I can't see our cars, then they won't have a problem! I really can't stand the tension of watching our cars. All I need to see is the race positions and car Numbers 5 and 6 clicking up the laps, preferably while leading. I'm just willing them to come past the pits each time and record another lap safely completed.'

The Longines timing screen made satisfactory reading as Coulthard (Number 6) and Hill (Number 5) competed 19 laps at the head of the field, the monitor showing that the Williams drivers were pulling away from the rest of the field. Hill made his first pit stop. Then it was Coulthard's turn. He failed to appear.

Gasps from onlookers in the Williams garage warned Ann that the television screen was bringing bad news. A quick glance showed David's car, its front suspension broken, parked against the wall at the entrance to the pit lane. Just as he was coming in, the engine revs had risen more rapidly than Coulthard had expected, forcing the car straight into the waiting concrete.

Ann concentrated on the timing monitor while waiting for Coulthard to return on foot. Television crews and reporters were already waiting to find out why the race leader had retired in such an unusual way. Meanwhile, Hill was pressing on and, with the passing of each lap,

■■■

the monitor was making extraordinary reading. The opposition was falling apart, Schumacher and Alesi colliding, Frentzen, Berger and Herbert retiring with mechanical trouble. Hill's lead extended to more than a minute. It was an unheard of luxury. And a useful one too.

Damon's third and final pit stop caused pulses to soar when a wheel nut jammed. He was delayed by more than ten seconds, but such was his advantage that he could have afforded to get out of the car and do the job himself without losing the lead.

Even so, as the final laps of a race which is notoriously tough on equipment began to count down, the tension mounted. The team wanted this win so badly; it would be cruel if Hill lost it now. David Brown was anxious for more than the obvious reasons. Tradition has it that anyone leaving a team receives rough treatment at the hands of his colleagues. Brown was half-expecting some horrible form of punishment even though Dickie Stanford, fearing that concern for his well-being might affect Brown's concentration, had promised that nothing would happen during the race. Stanford was true to his word. Just.

As the team stretched over the wall to welcome home an equally delighted Hill, Brown raised his fist in salute and then turned to leave the pit wall. He was met by a torrent of water and foam from all directions. By the time the boys had finished with him, Brown looked as though he had been dragged through a car wash. It set the scene for celebrations which would stretch into the small hours of Monday morning.

Ann Bradshaw, meanwhile, had rushed upstairs to the media centre, where she watched television pictures of the beaming winner accepting his trophy on the rostrum. Damon could not have been happier since he had dominated the weekend and this result would help vanquish the dissatisfaction which would otherwise have intruded on the four-month off-season. Hill was then ushered into the television studio, Bradshaw using her mini-tape recorder to capture quotes as Damon's voice boomed from the loudspeaker.

Three-quarters of an hour had passed by the time Hill had finished the television and media interviews. Had the race been in Europe, where the press would have been on a tight deadline, Bradshaw would have started work on the post-race press release. But, with time on the side of everyone bar the local media, Ann waited for Damon to make his way from the press centre. An attempt to hustle him down the staircase was scuppered by a television crew coming the other way and immediately conducting an interview. There was an immediate log-jam. No one seemed to mind.

Hill, followed by a jostling mixture of media and race

fans, finally reached the sanctuary of the garage to a round of applause from sponsors, guests and those team members who were not busy packing away equipment. The first person Damon saw was Brown, now cleaned up sufficiently to allow a back-slapping embrace for the final time with his driver.

In the office, Hill changed out of his driving suit and then phoned home. Just as he finished the conversation with Georgie, in walked George Harrison, the former Beatle who shares Hill's interest in motor racing and his love of rock music. Photographers, jostling at the door, finally spilled into the office. Harrison, shunning the limelight, quietly slipped away.

As mechanics, some wearing shirts swapped with members of rival teams, brought more mementos for signing, Hill picked up his crash helmet and, using a silver marker, inscribed a message before giving the dark blue helmet to Brown as a keepsake. Meanwhile, Ann Bradshaw was busy writing on a more official basis. The Williams press release summed up a perfect end to an imperfect year. Hill's quote read:

'I'm pleased for myself, for Adelaide and especially the Rothmans Williams-Renault team who have been through the mangle as much as I have this year. It's a funny old game, isn't it?'

ACKNOWLEDGEMENTS

Once again, in a year that has had its ups and downs, everyone at both track and factory has overcome their frustrations to enable me to go about my job. Thank you, and I hope you like it. **Jon Nicholson**

This book would not have been possible without the permission of Frank Williams and the cooperation of the entire team. To everyone at Williams-Renault, very many thanks. **Maurice Hamilton**

The Williams Team

John Alcon, Sean Allen, Pete Ampleford, Ian Anderson, Roger Andrews, Graham Appleton, Jim Barker, Derek Basey, Darren Beacroct, Jim Bennett, Ruth Berry, Stephen Berry, Keith Biddick, Kieron Blay, Steve Blewett, Nick Boccacci, Nicola Bonnin, Fleur Bosley, Steve Bradbury, Ann Bradshaw, Richard Brady, Ray Brannagan, Mike Brew, David Brown, Alan Broadhead, Preston Bulson, Simon Bunce, John Burridge, James Burton, David Byles, John Cadd, Brian Campbell, Robbie Campbell, Chris Carter, Ian Cartwright, Alan Challis, Colin Chapman, Hamish Charles, Sonia Chester, Jock Clear, Paul Clements, Irene Clibbon, Steve Coates, Alan Cole, Clive Cooper, Graham Cooper, Dave Copping, Matthew Croucher, Martin Crowder, Iain Cunningham, Bob Davis, Lisa Dickinson, Chris Dietrich, Scott Doe, Jim Douglas, Dave Dunn, Phil Ebberson, Paul Eden, Frances Edwards, Paul Edwards, Nigel Edwards, Nan Eldred, Steve Eldred, Terry Eldred, Teresa Eltham, Mick Emanuel, Phil Farrand, Gavin Fisher, Judd Flogdell, Pete

ACKNOWLEDGEMENTS

Fostekew, Bruce Foster, Steve Fowler, Stephen Fraser, Carl Gaden, Terry Galt, Bernie Goble, Jane Gorard, Jim Green, Matthew Green, Stephen Greenway, Mervyn Griffiths, Steve Hackwood, Eghbal Hamidy, Brian Hartigan, Steve Harvey, Dave Haste, Phil Hawke, Patrick Head, Chris Hessey, Colin Hessey, Chris Hessey, Mark Hicks, Chris Hiett, Martin Higgs, Brian Hillier, Robert Hillsdon, Ralph Holland, Tom Holman, Nigel Homes, Russell Hooton, Andy Hope, Mark Horspole, Jon How, Dave Hughes, Richard Iley, Mervyn Ingram, Leigh Janes, Bernie Jones, David Jones, Les Jones, Tim Judkins, David Juniper, Victoria King, Simon Lacey, Bryan Lambert, Dave Lang, Ian Lawlor, Mark Loasby, Dave Locke, Mick McCrowan, Andrew McDowell, Neil McKay, Alan Mann, Pete Marshall, Colin Martin, Duncan Mayall, David Miles, Drew Miller, Chris Mitchell, Mattion Mobbs, Phil Moore, Steve Morton, Kim Mulford, Stuart Mulley, Kieran Murphy, Chris Newcombe, Adrian Newey, Mas Nightingale, Lynn Nixon, Kevin O'Brien, Steve Oliver, Sean O'Mahony, Brian O'Rourke, Richard Osman, David Owen, Derek Page, Bob Paxman, Eddie Pearce, Ian Pearce, Simon Peters, Bryan Pettifer, Leigh Pettifer, Jean Pickard, Steve Pieri, Bryan Pigott, Tony Pilcher, Scott Pinnell, Richard Polley, Stewart Prattley, Tim Preston, Steve Prior, Barbara Przydatek, Brian Redpath, Jacqui Richardson, John Riordan, Donna Robertson, Stuart Roberton, Mark Saxon, John Saxton, Simon Scoins, Graham Searle, Alex Shaw, Andrew Smith, Bob Smith, Richard Smith, Dickie Stanford, Geoff Street, Ian Stubbs, Mark Sturdy, Maria Sullivan, John Sutton, Paul Symington, Jim Tait, Gordon Talbot, Nick Talbot, Jim Taylor, Chris Tee, Jonathan Tempest, Nolan Thompson, Paul Tinkler, Roger Tipler, Vincent Todd, Pat Tohill, Bob Torrie, Richard Townley, Grant Tuff, Robbie Tyers, Gwyn Upjohn, Les Wainwright, David

POLE POSITION

■■

Walker, Jim Walter, Basil Warner, Colin Watts, Hilary Weaver, Simon Wells, Paul West, Richard West, John Westwood, Chris Wheatley, Matthew Whyte, David Williams, Frank Williams, John Williams, Adrian Willis, Geoff Willis, John Wilson, Steve Wise, David Witham, Rex Woodley, Nigel Woods, Gary Woodward, Jim Wright, Peter Yonge, Alan Young, Paul Young.

And finally . . .

We would like to thank everyone at Macmillan for their help and hard work in making this book.

Official Williams Supporters Club membership details and hotline

Telephone 0181 421 6010   Fax: 0181 421 0475

■■